Replacing Americans

Replacing Americans

✦

The Deadly Consequences of an Open Border With Mexico

Dave Gibson and Laura Leighton

iUniverse, Inc.
New York Bloomington

Replacing Americans
The Deadly Consequences of an Open Border With Mexico

iUniverse books may be ordered through booksellers or by contacting:

iUniverse
1663 Liberty Drive
Bloomington, IN 47403
www.iuniverse.com
1-800-Authors (1-800-288-4677)

Because of the dynamic nature of the Internet, any Web addresses or links contained in this book may have changed since publication and may no longer be valid.

ISBN: 978-1-4401-9354-5 (sc)
ISBN: 978-1-4401-9355-2 (ebk)

Printed in the United States of America

iUniverse rev. date: 1/5/10

Foreword

By Laura Leighton

AMERICANS, WAKE UP! YOU ARE BEING REPLACED!

Most Americans are still trying to come to terms with how our nation has gotten to the point of bankruptcy, when just a few years ago we had an economic surplus. Or, how and why have so many Americans lost their jobs to cheap labor? Or why is an invasion by millions of people being allowed into this country with no serious attempt at stopping it?

Many of those same Americans are just coming to the realization that our government, whether it be Democrat or Republican, has been usurped by people who don't owe any allegiance to either our nation, nor our Constitution. These so-called leaders seem to be taking us down a path toward a One World Government or New World Order (dictatorship), as George Bush Sr. mentioned many years ago.

Of course, this takeover is not being reported by the mainstream media.

I am a daughter of immigrants and worked as a translator-interpreter and loved working with Hispanics. Out of the many languages I had studied, I chose Spanish to work with and spent over 30 years helping Hispanics to understand and to be understood. And I loved helping them, that is until I moved to Arizona. As a daughter of immigrants, I loved working with immigrants and refugees. I never knew about Mexico's agenda until I came to Arizona and began working at an organization that helps the indigent.

Part of what we did was help people who had "immigration" problems. "Immigration" usually refers to the system by which people can come legally into a nation to assimilate, and bring us the skills that a country may be lacking.

An immigration system screens people to make sure they have no criminal background and are in good health. It ensures that foreign criminals and deadly diseases do not enter the nation. The immigration system requires background checks and health checks in order to protect Americans. Those who are approved to come in are of good moral character and add to the nation.

But in this case, we were dealing with people who sneak and have no interest in applying to the nation, nor in waiting their turn. Or, they simply overstay their visas. These are not "immigrants" – these are "illegal aliens". There is a huge difference between "illegal aliens" and "immigrants."

For some reason, I found, the illegal aliens I interpreted for thought it was "ok" to break another country's laws and come and go as they pleased. I noted that the vast majority were from Mexico, and I never met one out of the thousands I interviewed over the years who had any respect for law. Many would tell me, "We don't follow laws in Mexico," and many would ask me how much it cost to bribe the judge or the prosecutor or their own attorney.

When I would tell them that "bribery" is not how Americans deal with their court cases, many would get angry!

Most of the illegal aliens I interpreted for were working in this country illegally. Later I found many of my friends had lost their jobs to illegals. Some of my friends were either fired or laid off from jobs they had had for a lifetime, but lost them to people who accepted very low wages with no benefits so they could get these jobs.

One American was losing his home and could not afford to put food on the table for his family. For 30 years, he worked paving roads but the last job for which he applied, the employer told him, "I can get two illegals for the price of you!" He could no longer find a job and gave up. An American not being able to work in his own country because big business wants cheap labor? What is wrong with this picture? And, why is our government allowing this?

One young fellow I interpreted for who found out he had impregnated his 19 year old girlfriend started to kick her in the stomach to make her abort when her father entered the room. He beat the father up, also, and was taken to jail. He asked me nonchalantly how much it cost to bribe the judge, the prosecutor and his attorney and when I told him he could not do that, he became angry.

I realized by this time that he was coming from a nation with a different set of values and customs.

A few years later, I noticed that the newspapers were not telling us everything that was going on - even major events and especially from around the nation. And that now our words were being manipulated.

They started by calling "illegal aliens" the respected word "immigrants". ("Illegal aliens" is the correct immigration term for someone who comes in violation of the law such as sneaking or overstaying one's visa). This purposeful misuse of the word "immigrant" is an insult to every immigrant who ever came to this country legally and who spent years waiting their turn.

Then we were told they were "just coming here to better themselves" (even though they were breaking the law), and had those "family values that don't end at the border." They did not tell us about all the cases of murder, rape, child abuse, etc., that illegal aliens were perpetrating. However, on the internet, I kept finding case after case of child molestation even down to tiny babies and the child molesters were almost always from Mexico.

Then I came across one of Dave Gibson's articles which described the cultural attitudes in Mexico, and the fact that young girls are often abused and raped but the men committing these crimes are almost never punished. In fact, it was in one of his articles that I learned that if a Mexican man who is accused of rape, offers to marry his victim, the judge usually dismisses the charges (the practice is known as 'rapto').

After I read more of Dave's articles which explained so much about illegal immigration and Mexico's role in the destruction of our country, I got in touch with him. And asked him to write this book with me.

You will be introduced to many disturbing aspects of this invasion, and as you read, you will understand the incredible detriment illegal immigration has become to this country and the motives behind it. And at the end, we present a chapter on "Solutions" which can help save this nation.

Americans need to realize that Mexico is NOT our friend as we have been told but our worst enemy!

Several years ago, one of Mexico's politicians was asked how Mexico was going to drain the U.S. of everything she has. He was asked, "How do you eat an elephant". (We are the elephant.) His reply: "One piece at a time."

Chapter 1

Mexican Time Bomb

The U.S. Census Bureau recently released data which shows that the United States population has reached 300 million. Illegal immigration from Mexico and Central America, and the rate at which they are giving birth in this country is fueling the population explosion.

In 2005, Latinos accounted for half of the U.S. population growth. Less than one-fifth of 2005's increase could be attributed to caucasian, natural-born Americans. According to calculations by the Census Bureau, a baby is born in the U.S. every eight seconds...more than likely its an Anchor Baby!

The widely known but always down-played Reconquista Movement is alive and well and coming to a town near you. Mexico is taking back much of this country through very aggressive illegal immigration as well as through equally aggressive breeding. The goal of the Reconquista Movement was once to take back the southwestern border states of California, New Mexico, Arizona, and Texas. However, illegal aliens and their offspring are now building colonies in every state of the union.

The following statistics provided by the U.S. Census Bureau are staggering and frightening:

The total U.S. population more than doubled from 131.7 million in 1940 to 290.8 million in 2003, the Latino population increased nearly 30 times in that same period. In 1940, the Latino population within the U.S. was 1.4 million, by 2003 it had swelled to 40 million.

Between 2000-2003, the Latino population within the U.S. grew at a rate of 13 percent, while the U.S. non-Latino population grew at a rate of only 0.8 percent during the same period.

The hyper-racist Latino group known as La Raza recently proudly reported on their website that 85 percent of the Latino population under 18 were born inside the United States. According to the U.S. Census Bureau, 80 percent of our Latino population is age 44 or younger, which means that the vast majority of Latinos in the U.S. are still of child-bearing age.

With the incredible birth rates of Latinos and the ongoing Mexican invasion, this country will become another Latin American nation in our lifetime. What will this mean to you?...The disappearance of the English language, the destruction of our traditional American culture, the over-population of our cities, epidemics of once-thought eradicated diseases, crushing poverty, and soaring crime. Considering the fact that illegal aliens already account for 30 percent of this nation's prison population --we can expect that prison building will become the new growth industry.

Imagine your suburban neighborhood filled with rooming houses, with several male illegal aliens in each one, or those now single-family homes inhabited by several Latino families. Picture your favorite deli or coffee shop replaced with a bodega. You can also kiss Chinese, Italian, and soul food restaurant goodbye. Don't believe it?...Try finding anything but Mexican food in an area dominated by Latinos. You see, unlike white Americans Latinos see no reason for multi-culturalism.

But the real problem will be that our politics will be controlled by those whose loyalty actually lies with another nation. Once our political system becomes dominated by Mexican-Americans, our resources will no longer be our own, but will be used only to benefit Mexico.

If an effort is not made to protect our border with Mexico and we do not soon adopt a sensible immigration policy--the United States as we know it will cease to exist in the near future.

Chapter 2

U.S Citizenship Or A Used Car?

Despite the defeat by the American people of the 2007 McCain/Kennedy Amnesty Bill, President Obama is now planning another attempt at amnesty for the millions of foreign nationals now residing in this country illegally.

We overwhelmingly rejected the bill and our legislators heard us in numbers never before seen. However, during the 2008 election, promises were made by both the Democrat and Republican nominees to pass the incredibly unpopular measure.

While the party faithful on both sides of the aisle claimed to offer a real alternative to the other, McCain's and Obama's support for amnesty provided proof that neither candidate actually planned to represent the will of the people.

Last year, Republican Presidential candidate John McCain told the crowd at the 2008 National La Raza Conference: "I don't want to fail again to achieve comprehensive immigration reform." Barack Obama also addressed La Raza and pledged his support for so-called comprehensive immigration reform.

Of course, "comprehensive immigration reform" is nothing more than code for amnesty for illegal aliens.

The amnesty bill written by McCain would have merely required illegal aliens to pay a $5,000 fee in order to stay here and gain legal residency. The fact that American citizenship is now valued at roughly the same cost as a 2003 Volkswagen is insulting, the fact that our own Congress and President have arrived at that estimation speaks to how little respect our elected representatives have for this nation.

3

Many believe that through his incompetent leadership, Bush helped throw the 2006 mid-term elections to the Democrats in order to rid the House of enough conservative Republicans to finally pass his amnesty plan. The once conservative House had been the only thing standing in the way of Bush and his plan to give "a path to citizenship" to millions of illegal aliens.

However, Bush did not anticipate the incredible activism displayed by the American people, who flooded the Senate with emails, letters, and phone calls. In fear for their political life, U.S. Senators changed their intended vote to "NO" on McCain's amnesty plan.

Now both the House and Senate are controlled by Democrats who have been in favor of a blanket amnesty plan for years. Seeking the Hispanic vote, Obama made it clear that he would sign such a plan, it would appear that the days are numbered for America's sovereignty.

We are all being sold-out and now we must watch as our precious citizenship will be offered for a $5,000 fee to anyone who invades our once sovereign soil. Senator John McCain who will never let us forget that he is a veteran, basically told us that the sacrifices made by all of the men who have fought and died for this nation meant nothing...Or at least no more than the blue book value of an '03 Jetta!

Anyone who sneaks into our country, will enjoy the same rights and privileges as those who wait for years to come here legally. I suppose, anyone who has trespassed on a rancher's property, cutting their fences and endangering their livestock will now be regarded in the same light as the brave souls who settled at Jamestown 400 years ago.

Under McCain's bill, even members of Mexican drug gangs would have received amnesty by simply signing a statement in which they renounced their gang affiliation, the so-called 'background checks' that illegal aliens would receive are only of the 24-hour variety, which reveal very little (if anything) and would then be given a six-month worker card. Even violent members of MS-13 would be given legal status based on nothing but their promise to become upstanding citizens.

My great-grandfather fought in World War I and sustained a grievous injury at the hands of the German Imperial Army, an injury which caused him to suffer for the rest of his long life. As I stare at his discharge papers and Victory Medal now proudly displayed above my desk, I wonder what he would think of this day. I wonder if he would now view the sacrifices he and so many of his comrades made for this nation to be pointless.

I grieve for my great-grandfather and for all of the courageous men who have taken up arms in defense of this great country. On this dark day, I grieve not only for the ones who are now gone but most of all for the veterans who are still here. The brave men who fought in bloody battles defending the American way of life, now must watch as those currently in power render their service irrelevant.

I would have never believed that a day would come when our Republic would be controlled by those willing to trade American citizenship for the promise of potential votes and cheap labor. However, that sad day is now upon us.

Chapter 3

Think Illegal Immigration Is A 'Victim-Less' Crime?...Not For This Girl's Family!

On March 30, 2007, in Virginia Beach, Va., a Mexican national named Alfredo Ramos slammed into the rear of a vehicle in which Allison Kuhnhardt, 17 and Tessa Tranchant, 16 were stopped, while waiting at a red light. Ramos, 22 was traveling at a high rate of speed and was drunk at the time. He actually had nearly a .20 blood-alcohol level and could barely see the police officers in front of him. The two high school students had to be cut from their crumpled car and both later died after being taken to the hospital. Ramos suffered only a busted lip.

Though an illegal alien, Alfredo Ramos had been living in Virginia Beach for quite a while and worked at a local Mexican restaurant known as Mi Casita. Ramos had been previously convicted of three separate charges of public intoxication, identity theft, and even a DUI, but continued to live in the area. He speaks only Spanish and required an interpreter at all of his court proceedings.

While Ramos had already been convicted of a DUI, Virginia Beach policy dictated that an illegal alien be convicted of three DUI's before police would report them to federal immigration authorities. Virginia Beach police have since taken a more active role in determining the citizenship of those they arrest.

Tessa Tranchant's brother Dylan had only been home from Iraq for two weeks, when his sister was killed. Dylan was tasked with identifying his little sister's body. The case gained national fame thanks to the reporting of Fox News' Bill O'Reilly.

Last year I interviewed Ray Tranchant, Tessa's dad. What follows is the text of that interview:

1)How are you and your family coping with this terrible loss?

It is the biggest challenge of my life. I have been through some hard but fun times being a retired Naval officer, Annapolis graduate, Aircraft Carrier aviator, public school teacher, and now College administrator. The challenges these career paths have taken me pale in comparison to losing a little girl.

If you have suffered a loss of someone close to you that is totally unexpected (death sometimes is more predictable with serious illnesses, age, or severe accidents), no matter what the reason, it is at first almost surreal.

My ex-wife Colette, Kelsey,15 and Dylan, 25 were swept with total emotion and grief immediately and I chose to compartmentalize and suppress my grief so that the task at hand (funeral arrangements, family, and my job) were taken care of. I suffer still, but need help from friends and God to cope. Colette still understandably breaks down a lot and Kelsey is angry about many things in life that I don't think would have bothered her if her sister were still alive. Dylan moved away from the area and chose to go to a College in Washington D.C. about 200 miles from Virginia Beach. He is an artist and will undoubtedly express himself with music and drawings. All of us are undergoing Therapy and need various medications.

2) What kind of kid was Tessa?

Tessa was a free spirit, and had many gifts, like emotional intelligence. She was very attractive and was everyone's friend (a social animal that got up at 4:00am in the morning to get ready for High School), a gifted Irish step dancer, and a good surfer, had a great voice, and tickled me with her laugh. She loved comedies; anything with Ben Stiller, Will Farrell, Dave Chappell, Mike Myers, and Borat.

When she smiled, my heart always skipped a beat. She was truly loved by everyone who spent any time with her.

She is buried next to her friend Ali Kunhardt in Princess Anne Memorial Park, next to a statue of an angel. I visit her every Friday, the night she was killed.

The crash site on Virginia Beach Blvd. continues to be a memorial by the community, it always has flowers, balloons, notes and pictures, and has for the past 1.5 years.

3) Are you angry with the local city governments for their role in allowing Ramos to stay in this country?

I am not angry but very disappointed that Ramos was not deported after two previous offenses. He admitted he was an illegal immigrant, admitted that he purchased a fake driver's license from Florida, and nearly killed a Chesapeake, Virginia police officer with a head-on collision the second time he was arrested. Judge Whitehurst from Chesapeake gave him a fine and he walked. His roommate, a woman with a small baby who shared an apartment out of convenience with Ramos, said essentially that Ramos was not worried or fazed with the Whitehurst hearing and continued to come home drunk every night. Apparently he wasn't worried about being deported or even the need to get sober, because he continued the same behavior, which ultimately killed Tessa and Ali.

I am disappointed at the way the municipalities, the Commonwealth, and the Federal Government interact with immigration issues. Enforcement varies from city to city and state to state, and all of the states that interact with ICE claim that they get no support once ICE is notified. Of course ICE want to do their job, but they are greatly outnumbered and don't have the funds to integrate criminal databases to catch criminal illegal offenders. Some of the illegals have been quoted as saying, after receiving jail time and even deportation: "don't worry. I'll be back!" What kind of finger pointing, "not my job" system have we created, or let's just say allowed to evolve into an unmanageable monster?

That's why I'm interested in holding them all accountable with a lawsuit that would ultimately hold their feet to the fire and standardize these strung out policies.

How can we have sanctuary cities or mayors of these cities that take the law into their own hands?

Like the Mayor of San Francisco who endorsed two juvenile illegal immigrants with drug offenses to be flown back to Honduras by the Mayor's administration? How can any man bypass federal law? Why aren't the politicians serving time for violating federal law? Who can answer this for me? I thought this was America, one land, one set of rules.

After Tessa and Ali's death many of the cities in Virginia changed their policy on asking the immigration status of people who are arrested. I am thankful for this, but it won't bring back Tessa. I sure hope it helps others from losing their children.

4) Have the circumstances of your daughter's death been accurately reported by the media?

I think the media has done a good job reporting the facts. I think that FOX News, O'Reilly, Glen Beck on MSNBC, and Laura Ingram on FOX were very gracious in letting me tell our story. When the deaths happened, Virginia Beach seemed more worried about the mudslinging with O'Reilly than admitting that the system was broken and change needed to be on the horizon. Even the Governor of Virginia has not come out with a policy on illegal immigration.

However Virginia's attorney general, who is elected and not appointed, has clarified the current law that allows local police departments to check and inquire about the immigration status of the arrestee. That is what it's like in a state where bi-partisan politics prevent a compromise or a solution to many public problems.

5) Did you ever see Alfredo Ramos display any remorse for his crime? And what would you say to him?

No and I have a feeling that is why Judge Shadrick gave him 40 years in prison.

6) How has this tragedy changed your life?

I am more compassionate with my fellow man, I walk and talk to God more often and with more conviction, and I try to look at the big picture more than I used to before the deaths. I try not to get bogged down with the small details that won't matter in the long run, and finally, I see how fragile life really is.

7) Have you become active in the debate over illegal immigration?

I am on the Congressional Alien Criminal Task Force with Rep's Drake, Cantor, Wittman and Forbes.

I have spoken on 3 national news shows about my views and hope to get more time.

8) Is there anything you would like to say to President Bush?

The Executive Branch, including the Attorney General, needs to enforce with clarity the current laws, which would require deportation of any illegal alien criminal.

They need to secure the borders with more than a structure. We secure (and I mean secure!) thousands of miles of top secret military installations in America (area 51 is a good example) with the most sophisticated electronics and sensors that allow the interceptors to pinpoint the intruders and concentrate air and ground assets to interdict swiftly.

Finally, Homeland Security and ICE can provide digital fingerprint databases to municipalities so when any person, including a suspected illegal, can be fingerprinted then identified by face, alias, and criminal record. If it is an illegal and they have committed a crime, arrest and deport them. Their ticket to America is over.

If theme parks like Bush Gardens, Williamsburg, can keep a digital fingerprint on file to verify your ticket, and entrance to the theme park is a fingerprint scan (they did this to 3.5 million visitors last year), I think the Government can do it as well!

9) What would you like to hear from candidates John McCain and Barack Obama?

That they will make an effort to stop the two major parties from bickering over the solution with a strong bi-partisan committee. Both parties are going to have to give and take.

One final thought: When the War is over, and some day it will be, what are we going to do with the upward of 100,000 troops that will be laid off just like the last Gulf War? The economy took a hiccup last time in the early 90's. I propose that we move a great deal of these troops to our borders and gradually let them go until they were completely secure. Border patrol would certainly be a welcome place compared to Iraq, and the troop strength would not diminish in case of need again. Also, protecting America is a good mission.

End.

I want to take the opportunity to once again publicly thank Ray Tranchant for taking the time to talk with me about this most painful and senseless loss. I told Ray that I too am a dad, and it was tough for me to even write out my questions to him. This story has deeply touched and angered me. This could happen to any family, anywhere in this country. Considering the obvious unwillingness of our elected officials to defend our border and remove illegal alien criminals from our cities, this type of tragedy will hit lots of folks.

The next time you hear someone make the claim that President Bush kept this country safe since 9/11, please remind them of 16 year-old Tessa Tranchant.

Chapter 4

Latin American Gangs Are Taking Over Our Streets

At one time, violent crimes attributed to Mexican and Central American gangs were largely confined to Los Angeles. However, just as illegal aliens have spread across this country, so too has a veritable crime wave. We are now experiencing the early stages of the most violent gang epidemic we have ever seen.

While L.A. may be ground zero for Latino gangs such as MS-13, other cities are being victimized as well, and not only by MS-13 and not only in large cities.

One of the most disturbing examples of organized gang activity took place last year in Fort Worth, TX.

On January 3, 2008, police in Fort Worth arrested several members of the Latino gang known as Varrio Central for forcing young girls into prostitution. Some of the girls being victimized were as young as 12 years old.

Diego Rodriguez, 19, and Martin Reyes, 17, were charged with aggravated kidnapping, trafficking of a person, and engaging in organized criminal activity. The names of three minors arrested were not released.

Varrio Central members would typically befriend the girls, get them high, and then take them to their regular customers. They would also drive them through apartment complexes, approaching men with the offer of sex with a teen-aged or pre-teen girl for a fee of $50.

According to Fort Worth Police, if a girl refused to comply, gang members would beat and sexually assault her and threaten her family with violence.

Fort Worth Police Lt. Ken Dean told the Associated Press: "The age of the victims and suspects is the surprising part of it. To have such young individuals in a somewhat organized business, a forced prostitution ring, is somewhat alarming and such a horrendous crime against the 12 to 16 year old girls."

As I stated earlier, Latin American gang activity is no longer isolated to large cities. A look at one relatively small city reveals the severity of the problem.

According to 2007 U.S. Census Bureau statistics, the city of Porterville located in central California has a population of 51,467. While reporting a rather modest population, Porterville police report the existence of no less than 23 active gangs in the city.

The known gangs in Porterville, CA are as follows:

-Brown Pride Surenos
-Barrio Sur Trece
-Court Street Locos
-Mexican Gang Bangers
-North Side Varrio Boys
-Tierras-Terra Bella
-Tiny Maltido Surenos
-Varrio Central Poros
-Wicked Ass Surenos
-Young Mexican Gang Bangers
-Barrio "H" street
-Big Time Locos
-North Side Varrio Youngsters
-Sultra 14
-Varrio Campo Linnel
-West Side Poros
-Catela Norte
-East Side Poros
-East Side Varrio
-Sureno Life Style
-Richgrove Varrio Trece

The U.S. Justice Department now believes that many gangs never before associated with traditional Mexican gangs are now distributing drugs on behalf of Mexican drug cartels. These gangs include the Bloods, Crips, and even many Asian and white supremacist gangs.

The National Drug Intelligence Center recently reported that Mexican gangs now have drug distribution operations in North Carolina as well as Georgia to support drug sales along the East Coast.

In addition to the sale of illegal drugs, prostitution, assault, rape, and robbery, Latin American gangs are now apparently acting as paid assassins, with the target being U.S. law enforcement.

In 2007, the Inland Valley Daily Bulletin reported that they had obtained a confidential Department of Homeland Security memo. The function of the document was to issue an Officer Safety alert to U.S. Border Patrol agents that human smugglers were bringing MS-13 gang members into the country for the sole purpose of murdering the agents.

The alert reads: "Unidentified Mexican alien smugglers are angry about the increased security along the U.S./Mexican border and have agreed that the best way to deal with U.S. Border Patrol agents is to hire a group of contract killers."

A Border Patrol agent speaking on the condition of anonymity said: "It's not just people coming over here to pick lettuce. These gang members, criminals, are endangering American lives." He went on: "Our vests won't stop a rifle bullet, and many of us feel like sitting ducks."

A few facts concerning the impact of illegal immigration on crime in this country:

-In 1995, a California Department of Justice study concluded that the 18th Street Gang works directly with the Mexican Mafia, and commits a robbery or an assault every day in Los Angeles alone.

-Two-thirds of fugitive felony warrants issued in Los Angeles are for illegal aliens.

-95 percent of warrants issued for murder in L.A. are for illegal aliens.

-83 percent of warrants issued for murder in Phoenix, AZ are for illegal aliens.

-86 percent of warrants issued for murder in Albuquerque, NM are for illegal aliens.

-53 percent of burglaries in Nevada, New Mexico, Arizona, California, and Texas are committed by illegal aliens.

-According to police, there are at least 53,000 Latino gang members in Los Angeles (that is the equivalent of three Airborne divisions).

-Mexican drug cartels produce 80 percent of the methamphetamine sold on U.S. streets.

-In 2007 alone, U.S. Customs agents confiscated over 2,000 lbs of methamphetamine at the six official border crossing stations in California.

Latin American gangs are just another reason to vigorously defend our all-too porous border. If our government does not soon become serious about border enforcement, we can expect our nation's streets to soon run red with blood.

Chapter 5

Our Police Officers Are Paying the Ultimate Price For An Open Border

Despite the false rhetoric spilling from the mouths of our politicians, not every illegal immigrant comes here simply to work. In fact, many of them come here to cause mayhem in our streets. One consequence of illegal immigration is the murder of many U.S. police officers.

The following is a look at a few of those slain officers:

On Sept. 30, 1992, Oregon State Trooper Bret Clodfelter, 34 stopped a suspected drunk driver who turned out to be an illegal alien named Francisco Manzo-Hernandez. The drunken driver was traveling with two of his fellow invaders. Trooper Clodfelter handcuffed the driver and placed him in the back seat of his cruiser.

As all of the men were drunk, the state trooper offered to drive the two passengers home. For his kindness, Clodfelter was shot in the head four times. All three fled the scene and were captured a few days later.

Trooper Clodfelter served with the Oregon State Police for eight years and left behind a wife, son, and daughter. A further tragedy took place a year after the trooper's murder, when his wife Rene, took her own life.

On March 26, 1999, Phoenix Police Officer Marc Atkinson, 28 was shot and killed by illegal alien Felipe Petrona-Cabana. Officer Anderson was ambushed by Cabana while on routine patrol. Cabana was traveling with two other illegal aliens and carrying a pound of cocaine. An armed citizen named Rory Vertigan witnessed the shooting and helped capture the outlaws.

Officer Atkinson served on the Phoenix Police Department for five years. He left behind a wife and an infant son.

On April 29, 2002, Los Angeles Sheriff's Deputy David March, 33 was shot to death by Mexican national Armando Garcia. Invader Garcia told friends that he wanted to kill a police officer. Garcia saw Deputy March on patrol one evening and pulled over and waited for March to drive past him. As soon as March began to pass, Garcia opened fire. Garcia fled back across the border after murdering March.

For four years, the government of Mexico refused to apprehend or extradite Garcia. In February 2006, U.S. Customs officers arrested Garcia in Mexico. Garcia has since pleaded guilty and was sentenced to life in prison.

Deputy March served with the Los Angeles Sheriff's Department for seven years and left behind a wife and stepdaughter.

On August 9, 2002, U.S. Park Ranger Kris Eggle, 27 was killed by Mexican drug dealers while on duty in Arizona's Organ Pipe Cactus National Monument Park. Ranger Eggle was attempting to apprehend two drug dealers, after being notified by Mexican authorities that the two had crossed the border and were headed into the park. One of the drug dealers opened fire on Ranger Eggle with an AK-47. Eggle died before a medivac helicopter arrived on the scene. Mexican police officers shot and killed Eggle's murderer.

U.S. Park Ranger Eggle left behind his grieving parents and his sister (also a U.S. Park Ranger).

On November 13, 2005, Dallas Police Officer Brian Jackson , 28 was shot to death by illegal alien Juan Lizcano. Officer Jackson responded to a call from Lizcano's ex-girlfriend. Lizcano was threatening her and fired a gun inside her house. As Officer Jackson approached the house, Lizcano fled at which time Jackson gave chase. Lizcano eventually lay in wait and fired on the Dallas patrolman. Officer Jackson died one hour later at Baylor Medical Center.

Juan Lizcano had been arrested two months before murdering the police officer (once for threatening his girlfriend with a knife and again for a DUI). Lizcano had been living illegally in the United States for two years.

Officer Brian Jackson served on the Dallas Police Department for five years. He left behind a wife of only two months.

On September 21, 2006, Houston Police Officer Rodney Johnson, 40 was shot and killed while making a routine traffic stop. The man that murdered Ofc. Johnson was a Mexican national who had been deported seven years earlier. However, President Bush's refusal to defend the Mexican border allowed this human predator to easily re-enter the United States and eventually turn this police officer's wife into a widow.

Officer Johnson stopped a commercial vehicle traveling 20 miles over the posted speed limit. The truck was driven by Juan Leonardo Quintero. A co-worker and Quintero's two stepdaughters were also in the vehicle.

When Quintero was unable to provide any form of identification, Ofc. Johnson handcuffed him and placed him in the backseat of his patrol car. Once the officer was seated behind the wheel again, Quintero though handcuffed, removed the 9mm handgun concealed in his waistband and began firing at Johnson through the plastic shield separating the front and back seats. Ofc. Johnson was shot in the head five times. He was pronounced dead shortly after being taken to a local hospital.

Officer Johnson was a 12 year veteran of the Houston Police Department and a U.S. Army veteran. While serving on the HPD, Johnson received two Lifesaving Awards. He left behind his wife Joslyn (also a police officer) and five children.

Clara Rodriguez, who lives in the neighborhood where Johnson patrolled had this to say about the murdered officer: "He was just so very nice. He was not ever mean. It just breaks my heart. I feel so very bad for his wife. He got up and went to work this morning, and this is what happened. This is what happened to one of the people who protects us, who truly took care of us."

Juan Leonardo Quintero is a convicted child molester and DWI offender, and was deported to Mexico by U.S. immigration officials in 1999. He had been working for a Houston area landscaping company and despite the DWI conviction, Quintero was driving a company vehicle at the time Officer Johnson stopped him.

These are only a few of the stories which illustrate the human cost of illegal immigration. The next time you hear someone say "they are only here to work"...Remember these police officers who paid the ultimate price for so-called cheap labor.

Chapter 6

Our Children Are Being Hunted By Illegal Aliens

Contrary to what President Bush often claimed, family values do stop at the Rio Grande for many illegal aliens. In addition to suppressing wages, bankrupting our hospitals, and over-crowding our jails and public schools, illegal aliens are preying upon our children

In Operation Predator sweeps across the country conducted between 2003-2007, Immigration and Customs Enforcement agents nabbed over 10,700 foreign national child molesters. Many of these predators had been previously convicted of other crimes, and many had already been deported once. The number of predators apprehended in the sweeps actually only represent the tip of the iceberg.

In fact, a study conducted by the Violent Crimes Institute reports that between 1999 and 2006, there were nearly 1,000,000 sex crimes committed in the United States by illegal aliens.

Using U.S. Department of Justice, Immigration, as well as state and local law enforcement data, Deborah Schurman-Kauflin of the Violent Crimes Institute determined that there are no less than 240,000 illegal alien sex offenders currently inside the U.S.

A very cursory search on the subject of illegal aliens committing acts of child molestation turned up countless examples of the growing problem. The following are two recent ones:

On April 17, 2009, Judge Cecil Puryear in Lubbock, TX, sentenced illegal alien and Mexican national Julian Vasquez to 15 years in prison for a July 2008 incident in which Vasquez broke into an apartment and sexually assaulted a 13-year-old girl.

Vasquez forced his way into the dwelling located in Cora Apartments, and shoved the girl onto the bed, tore off her shirt and bra, and fondled her breasts, according to court documents.

The girl was able to fight off Vasquez and ran into the bathroom, where she was able to call 911. When officers arrived, they found Vasquez still trying to open the bathroom door.

The only defense offered by Vasquez's attorney, Jesse Mendez, was that his client was drunk when he committed the frightening assault.

Lubbock County prosecutor Jennifer Basset told reporters: "This is an appropriate sentence for a stranger who broke into a house to molest a child. And this is a case where the effects on this child will not be forgotten by her, and this is a serious crime in Lubbock County."

On April 14, 2009, illegal alien and Salvadoran national Isaac Mendez Ramirez, 24 was arrested in Largo, FL and charged with two counts of capital sexual battery.

Ramirez is accused of molesting a 7-year-old girl in November 2008 and again in January 2009. According to the arrest report, Ramirez lives with the little girl but is not related to her. He is being held in the Pinellas County Jail.

In 2007, Americans For Legal Immigration Political Action Committee (ALIPAC) tracked child sexual assaults committed by illegal aliens. In a 30 day period, they recorded 27 assaults by foreign nationals illegally inside the United States. The results are as follows:

July 28, 2007
Milwaukee, Oregon
Charged: Alejandro Emetrio "Alex" Rivera Gamboa, 24, and Gilberto Javier Arellano-Gamboa, 23
Charges: rape and murder
Victim: Dani Countryman of Texas (15 years old)

August 6, 2007
Trenton, N.J.
Charged: Jose Carranza, 28
Charges: child rape (later charged with murder of Newark teenagers as well)
Victim: child's name withheld

August 16, 2007
Huron, Ohio
Charged: Lucio Sanchez-Martinez
Charge: gross sexual imposition of a minor
Victim: 8 year old girl

August 20, 2007
Oregon City, Oregon
Charged: Alejandro Hernandez-Flores, 19 and Mario Alberto
Flores-Estrada, 20
Charges: rape, sodomy, and sexual abuse
Victims: two girls ages 14 and 15

August 21, 2007
Franklin County, Alabama
Charged: Alvaro Vargas, 38
Charge: rape, sexual abuse
Victim: 11 year old girl

August 23, 2007
Bryan County, Oklahoma
Sought/Charged: Jose Retana
Charge: rape by instrumentation
Victim: 4 year old girl

August 24, 2007
Indianapolis, Indiana
Charged: Jesus Valenzuela, 19
Charges: child molestation and burglary
Victim: 5 year old girl

August 27, 2007
McAllen, Texas
Charged: Jorge Alberto Escobar
Charge: aggravated kidnapping
Victim: 5 year old girl

August 27, 2007
Rockville, Maryland
Sought/Charged: Mahumbo Kanneh, 23
Charges: rape, sexual assault, and molestation (Dismissed due to
lack of interpreter!)
Victims: 18 month and 7 year old girls

August 15, 2007
Indiantown, Florida
Charged: Ruben Hernandez-Juarez, 52
Charge: battery on a child for molesting
Victim: 6 year old boy

August 8, 2007
North Hollywood, California
Charged: Chalearmchai Nopthaisong, 41
Charges: kidnapping and lewd acts on a child
Victims: seven children (Police have since discovered six more
victims ranging from age 4 to 8 years old.)

July 20, 2007
Tulsa, Oklahoma
Charged: Daniel P. Ramirez, 39
Charges: sexual battery
Victim: 16 year old boy

August 14, 2007
Portsmouth, Massachusetts
Charged: Marvin Hernandez, 27
Charges: sexual assault
Victim: 14 year old girl

August 20, 2007
Gaston County, North Carolina
Charged: Ramon Zamora-Solano, 41
Charges: kidnapping and sexual assault
Victims: 5 and 6 year old girls

August 9, 2007
Poway, California
Charged: Jesus Mora Nava, 30
Charges: sexual assault
Victim: 13 year old boy

August 22, 2007
Palm Bay, Florida
Charged: Dwayne Modeste, 19
Charges: rape (armed with a machete)
Victims: 13 year old girl and 20 year old woman

August 20, 2007
Manchester, New Hampshire
Charged: Alan Hernandez, 18
Charges: sexual assault and criminal threatening
Victim: 14 year old girl

August 18, 2007
Brewster, New York
Charged: Sergio Antonio Martinez-Garza, 32
Charges: two felony counts of sexual conduct against a child
Victims: two girls ages 10 and 11

August 18, 2007
Brewster, New York
Charged: Pedro Sagastume, 21
Charges: rape
Victim: 13 year old girl

August 18, 2007
Brewster, New York
Charged: Jeremias Perez, 22
Charges: rape
Victim 15 year old girl

July 28, 2007
Tacoma, Washington
Charged: Terapon Adhahn, 42
Charges: rape, kidnapping, and murder
Victim: Zina Linnik, 12

July 30, 2007
Murfreesboro, Tennessee
Charged: Jesus G. "Egg" Garay-Barrientos, 18
Charges: aggravated sexual battery and rape
Victim: 6 year old girl

July 27, 2007
Alto, Texas
Charged: Eleazar Posadas, 49
Charges: indecent contact with a child
Victim: 7 year old girl

July 21, 2007
Village of Monroe, New York
Charged: Armando Sierra, 22
Charges: statutory rape
Victim: 14 year old girl

August 16, 2007
Bentonville, Arkansas
Charged: Daniel Lopez Bibiano, 34
Charges: attempted rape, sexual assault, and rape
Victims: 5, 10, 12, 13, and 15 year old girls

August 18, 2007
Indianapolis, Indiana
Charged: Israel Baez
Charges: In custody on other charges. Approached a group of children and arrested with a 'rape kit' in his van.
Witnesses: 5 children

So why does the crime of child molestation seem to be so prevalent among illegal aliens from Mexico?...The answer may lie within the age-old Mexican culture of "machismo," as well as within the actual laws of that country.

The crime of rape or child molestation is incredibly under-reported in Mexico, because there is so much shame placed upon the victim as well as the difficulty in proving the case. A 2002 Pulitzer Prize winning Washington Post article, reporter Mary Jordan detailed the case of a 16 year old Mexican girl who had reported being raped by three policemen in 1997. When Yessica Yadira Diaz Cazares and her mother went to the police station to report the rape, she was laughed at by the officers and actually jailed overnight.

Diaz was forced by police to undergo a medical exam as well as a total of eight blood tests. She was told that the blood tests would determine whether or not she had actually been raped. Prosecutors told the girl that she must physically put her hand on the men who raped her, courageously she proceeded even as the family received death threats.

The accused officer laughed at her and verbally abused the girl as she identified him as an attacker. Eventually, Yessica realized that justice would never be served and simply gave up. Sadly, she not only gave up her search for justice but her life as well. Despondent, she committed suicide by taking an overdose of prescription pills.

After Yessica's death, the national human rights commission pursued the case, resulting in the conviction of two of the accused officers.

The crime of kidnapping a woman for the purpose of rape and marriage against their will, or "rapto" as it is known in Mexico is actually a minor crime and rarely ever prosecuted. A Mexican legislator actually called the practice "romantic." Of course, this crime if committed in the United States would elicit felony charges and a penalty of 20 years to life in prison.

While rape is a serious crime in the United States, many Mexican nationals cannot understand why they are prosecuted on this side of the border. Often, a small payment of $10 to $20 to the victim's family will settle the matter back in Mexico.

The most troubling and telling reason behind the growing epidemic of child molestation at the hands of Mexican illegal aliens, is the fact the age of sexual consent throughout the majority of Mexico is 12 years of age!

The only other nation in the world which boasts such a disregard for childhood innocence is Zimbabwe, where the age of consent is also 12.

Article 177 of the Mexican Federal District Penal Code discusses "sexual abuse" and punishment of other acts referred to as "unintentional" acts –"who without purpose of reaching copulation, performs a sexual act with a person under 12 or a person that has no capacity of understanding the meaning of the act or that for any reason cannot resist it, or that demands that such act is observed or performed, will be punished with 2 to 7 years in prison".

In addition to Mexico City, the age of consent is 12 years old in the following Mexican states:

-Aquascalientes
-Baja California Sur
-Campeche
-Coahuila
-Guanajuato
-Guerrero
-Hidalgo
-Jalisco
-Michoacan
-Morelos
-Nayarit
-Oaxaca
-Puebla
-San Louis Potosi
-Sonora
-Tabasco
-Tamaulipas
-Yucatan
-Zacatecas

The age of consent is 13 years old in Nuevo Leon and 14 years old in the seven remaining Mexican states.

The attitude towards having sex with little girls is carried with many Mexican men as they cross into this country.

An example of this attitude can be found in Mexican national Diego Lopez-Mendez, who pled guilty in 2006 to sexually assaulting a 10 year old West Virginia girl. Through an interpreter, he told the court: "In the pueblo where I grew up girls are usually married by 13 years old....I was unaware of the nature of the offense or that it was a bad crime."

In order to bring charges of rape in most Mexican states, the law requires that the girl prove that she is a virgin, and that the charge of statutory rape be dropped if the rapist wishes to marry his victim.

Of course, when discussing the issue of illegal immigration, this dirty little secret is never talked about by our politicians, nor is the impact that such an attitude towards the abuse of children could have on this nation by offering amnesty to millions of Mexican nationals.

The next time someone tells you that illegal immigration is a 'victimless crime,' remind them of the children whose lives will never be the same.

Until our politicians gain the courage to actually defend our border...Keep your children close!

Chapter 7

The American People Deserve
An Investigation of Former U.S.
Attorney Johnny Sutton

Though he was sworn to protect the American people, it could easily be argued that recently retired U.S. Attorney Johnny Sutton operated more as an agent for the corrupt Mexican government, than as an advocate for the American people.

Since taking office, Sutton persecuted American law enforcement officers when they dared to defend our border or block the path of drug smugglers. Undoubtedly, Sutton's actions through his position as a U.S. Attorney, has greatly contributed to the growing violence being perpetrated by drug gangs on both sides of the border.

Johnny Sutton first caught the eye of George W. Bush in the early 1980's. At the time, Sutton was playing baseball for the NCAA National Champion Texas Longhorns and Bush was enjoying his role as a shareholder in the Texas Rangers organization. The two became fast friends and began a relationship that has benefited both men ever since.

Before being nominated by President Bush as U.S. Attorney for the Western District of Texas in 2001, Sutton served as a Policy Coordinator for the Bush-Cheney Transition Team, as well as the Criminal Justice Policy Director for Gov. Bush from 1995-2000.

In his time as U.S. Attorney, Sutton ruined the lives of several diligent and dedicated law enforcement officers who were working to defend our country from terrorists, illegal aliens, and drug smugglers. The following is a list of those brave men:

Border Patrol Agent Gary Brugman was charged by Sutton with violating the rights of an illegal alien in January 2001. The following year he was convicted and spent two years in federal prison.

Agent Brugman was working in the very tough border region of Eagle Pass, Texas. He responded to a scene where another agent was having trouble with a group of 10-12 apprehended people caught crossing our border illegally. Two of them would not comply, so Agent Brugman pushed one of the men onto the ground. This minor incident was enough for Sutton to charge Brugman with violating the illegal alien's constitutional rights "under the color of law." During Brugman's trial, Sutton actually brought a convicted drug smuggler whom Agent Brugman had arrested from his prison cell to testify against him.

Incredibly, Johnny Sutton did an interview on the Spanish language network Univision in which he stated he was making an example out of Agent Brugman.

In addition to his service as a Border Patrol agent, Brugman is a Coast Guard veteran. He spent 16 years of his life defending this nation. He is now free and actively telling his story in hopes that justice will soon come to Johnny Sutton.

Recently released U.S. Border Patrol Agents Ignacio Ramos and Jose Alonso Compean were sentenced to 11 and 12 year federal prison sentences respectively. Sutton charged these two men with assault with a deadly weapon, various firearms charges, and with violating a drug smuggler's civil rights.

In February 2005, Agents Ignacio Ramos and Jose Alonso Compean spotted a van headed across the border into the United States. The agents gave chase and one of them ended up in a scuffle with a Mexican drug smuggler known as Osvaldo Aldrete-Davila. One of the agents saw a gun in the smuggler's hand and fired at him, before Aldrete-Davila fled back across the border into Mexico. The smuggler was shot in the buttocks and was observed jumping into an awaiting vehicle on the Mexican side of the border.

The van driven by the smuggler was left behind along with 743 pounds of marijuana. A few months later, he was caught once again smuggling drugs into this country. While in custody, he was given immunity from prosecution in both cases in exchange for his testimony against Agents Ramos and Compean. In addition to immunity, the taxpayers assisted him with travel expenses and provided him with medical treatment at a U.S. Army facility in Texas. Once Aldrete-Davila testified and completed his medical treatments, he promptly filed a $5 million lawsuit against the U.S. Border Patrol for violating his rights.

Sutton's office has received a great deal of public criticism for his treatment and unfair prosecution of these two agents, while Rep. Duncan Hunter (R-CA) led a Republican movement in Congress to pardon these two men. Of course, president Bush commuted the sentences of Ramos and Compean on his last day of office. However, the felony conviction remains on their records and the two men can no longer work in law enforcement.

When Deputy Gilmer Hernandez made a routine traffic stop in April 2005, little did he know that this incident would lead to the loss of his freedom. It turned out that the driver was a human smuggler with several Mexican nationals hiding in the vehicle. After being approached, the driver hit the gas and tried to run over Dep. Hernandez. The deputy fired his weapon at the tires of the van, at which time a bullet fragment hit a woman who was hiding in the back of the vehicle, her injuries were limited to a scratch on the cheek. Another person in the van received a similar injury.

The shooting was investigated by the Edwards County Sheriff's Department, The Bureau of Alcohol, Tobacco and Firearms, as well as the Texas Department of Public Safety. All of the agencies deemed the action taken by Deputy Hernandez as justifiable. However, more than a year later, Sutton reopened the case and prosecuted Deputy Hernandez for violating the civil rights of the two injured illegal aliens. Hernandez served a one year sentence in a federal prison.

Border Patrol Agent Noe Aleman and his wife adopted his wife's nieces from Mexico, after the girls' father died. The couple paid $40,000 in legal fees to adopt the girls ages 12, 13, and 15. Despite the steep fees, the attorney they hired was apparently incompetent and made several errors on the adoption and immigration forms. Agent Aleman himself pointed out these errors to immigration authorities and attempted to correct them. For his honesty, Agent Aleman was arrested and prosecuted by Sutton's office for alien smuggling. He received a one year sentence and was incarcerated in the same prison where Agent Ramos was initially held.

Noe Aleman served with the Border Patrol for 12 years and is highly respected for his aggressive pursuits of illegal aliens and drug smugglers alike. However, in an effort to defame Agent Aleman, Johnny Sutton even suggested that the real purpose for the adoption was so that Aleman could molest the little girls, who during the grand jury hearing were referred to by Sutton's assistant as "little whores!"

In 2007, Aleman told Jerome Corsi of WorldNetDaily: "I'm just another victim in George Bush, Alberto Gonzalez, and Johnny Sutton's war against Border Patrol agents."

The three girls were sent to an orphanage in Mexico, after being deported.

There is evidence in two of these cases that the Mexican government became directly involved and influenced Sutton's office to prosecute the officers.

On March 4, 2005, the U.S. Consulate in Mexico contacted Sutton's office with information given by the Mexican government that they had a drug smuggler who had been shot by a Border Patrol Agent. The Department of Homeland Security began their investigation of Agents Ramos and Compean the very same day!

On April 18, 2005, Mexican Consul Jorge Ernesto Espejel Montes sent a letter to Sutton's office demanding that Deputy Gilmer Hernandez be prosecuted for injuring Maricela Rodriguez Garcia (the woman whose cheek was scratched while hiding in the smuggler's van). It was not until Sutton received this letter that his investigation of Dep. Hernandez began.

It would seem that U.S. Attorney Johnny Sutton received his orders directly from the corrupt government of Mexico. Sutton has not only punished several law enforcement officers for their efforts to protect this nation, but he has betrayed the American people as well.

Johnny Sutton's Western Texas District comprised over 660 miles of the U.S.-Mexican border. During Sutton's tenure, you can rest assured that every Mexican drug cartel knew that stretch of border to be the safest way to bring their drugs into the U.S.

If the Obama administration is truly serious about stamping-out government corruption and changing the culture of Washington, they will direct the Justice Department to open an investigation of former U.S. Attorney Johnny Sutton.

Chapter 8

The Mexican Military Regularly Enters This Country On Behalf of Drug Dealers

In August 2008, a Mexican military contingent held at gunpoint a U.S. Border Patrol agent. The incident occurred well inside the U.S. border, about 100 miles southwest of Tucson. The Mexican soldier eventually released the agent and returned to Mexico.

Shortly after the standoff, union Local 2544 of the National Border Patrol Council posted the following statement on their website: "Unfortunately, this sort of behavior by Mexican military personnel has been going on for years. They are never held accountable, and the United States government will undoubtedly brush this off as another case of 'Oh well, they didn't know they were in the United States.'

In January 2008, the Department of Homeland Security reported that since 1996, there had been 278 known incursions by the Mexican military into the United States. They are often seen providing armed escort to drug smugglers. Incredibly, the Mexican military now enters our nation at will, with no response from the U.S. government.

Last year, active-duty members of the Mexican military went much farther than simply escorting smugglers across our border. They broke into a home in Phoenix firing more than 100 rounds, resulting in the death of the homeowner.

In the early morning hours of June 22, 2008, six men wearing helmets, body armor, and Phoenix Police raid shirts and armed with AR-15's broke into the home at 8329 W. Cypress St. and shot and killed the resident, Mr. Andrew Williams. Phoenix police arrested three of the men, while the other three are still on the run. The three arrested and charged with first-degree murder are Manual Garcia-Trejo, Daniel Garcia-Saenz, and Rodolfo Madrigal Lopez, all are Mexican nationals.

One police report, which describes the crime reads: "Information from one of the suspects on McDowell indicated all the suspects are Mexican military coming into the United States with full tactical gear and police raid shirts to conduct home invasions. According to the same suspect, they were planning on ambushing the officers following them but didn't only because they didn't have any ammunition left."

That was the first known Mexican military or paramilitary raid carried-out in the interior of the United States. Until then, this type of activity has been confined to the border areas.

For some time it has been common knowledge among law enforcement that units of the Mexican military operate independently of Mexico City, and act as paid mercenaries and escorts on behalf of the Mexican drug cartels.

In early 2006, a typical example of these disturbing incidents took place along the Texas-Mexico border. On January 23, Hudspeth County deputy sheriffs came upon a gang of drug smugglers operating alongside a Mexican military unit. When confronted by the deputies, the Mexican soldiers retreated to their Humvee and "took up a defensive position," said Sheriff Arvin West.

The smugglers headed back across the river into Mexico. As one of their trucks became stuck in the water, the group unloaded the drugs and placed them into another vehicle. While this took place, the Mexican soldiers kept their rifles trained on the deputies. The truck still partially submerged, was then set ablaze.

Of course the Mexican government denied that any members of the military were involved in the affair. The U.S. State Department promised to conduct an investigation into the matter, the results of which have never been reported.

Shortly after that incident, a Border Patrol agent speaking on the condition of anonymity told the Inland Valley Bulletin: "We've had armed showdowns with the Mexican Army. These aren't just ex-military guys. These are Mexican army officials assisting drug smugglers."

In 2006, Chief of the U.S. Border Patrol David Aguilar testified before a Congressional Subcommittee that a run-in with the Mexican military "isn't a new phenomenon." He went on to say that U.S. Border Patrol agents often pursue and detain Mexican soldiers.

Also in 2006, the Department of Homeland Security released a document on the matter of Mexican military incursions into the U.S. which listed the following number of incidents within several Border Patrol sectors:

-San Diego County...17
-El Centro...58
-Tucson, AZ...39
-Yuma, AZ...24
-Del Rio, TX...3
-Marfa, TX...8
-El Paso, TX...33
-Rio Grande Valley, TX...28

Upon reviewing those troubling statistics, Rep. Tom Tancredo (R-CO) said: "It's a military problem. We should commit the military to the border tomorrow. I mean with armor and weapons."

Of course, President Bush announced in 2006 that he was sending National Guard units to the Mexican border to assist with border enforcement. However, before issuing the order, he placed a phone call to then Mexican President Vicente Fox, to reassure him that he was not "militarizing the border."

Bush made good on his promise to Fox with the apparent hamstrung rules of engagement under which the Guardsmen were operating.

On January 3, 2007, an armed paramilitary group of six to eight men, crossed the border into the United States and overran a National Guard post located near Sasabe, AZ. The Guardsmen from Tennessee quickly packed up their equipment, jumped into their truck, and fled the scene. That sorry action by the Guardsmen clearly demonstrated what our president instructed them to do...NOTHING!

Tennessee National Guard spokesman Randy Harris told the Associated Press: "The soldiers did exactly what their mission was, to pull back if they're approached by armed personnel coming across the border."

In an award ceremony which was closed to the press, the Tennessee National Guardsmen involved were presented with achievement medals for their actions described by their spokesman as a "tactical retreat."

The office of then Gov. Janet Napolitano (D-AZ) released a report to the Associated Press which praised the Tennessee National Guard unit for fleeing the scene in the face of an armed incursion into the United States. The report said: "We see this as a triumph of the training, discipline, and professionalism of the Guardsmen performing their mission."

With the two-year imprisonment of Border Patrol Agents Ramos and Compean for their aggressive pursuit of a Mexican drug smuggler, and National Guardsmen being rewarded for retreating from Mexican raiding parties, and Barack Obama's unwillingness to seal the border even under threat of a flu pandemic, it is obvious that our federal government will no longer defend the American people.

In 2008, speaking on this problem, Rep. Dana Rohrabacher (R-CA) said: "our president has chosen the side of our enemy. " While he was speaking about Bush, that sentiment would apparently apply to Obama as well.

It is more than maddening to know that we have a president who is willing to sit by and watch as a foreign military regularly enters this country, in the assistance of drug smugglers, and now even carries out murders in our neighborhoods.

A country which fails to defend their borders and sovereignty is not a country at all.

Chapter 9

The Drug Cartels Will Soon Be In Complete Control Of Mexico...Is The U.S. Next?

In the summer of 2008, Villa Ahumada Police Chief Jesus Blanco Cano was shot to death after only one day on the job. The town is located in the northern Mexican state of Chihuahua which is the territory of the very violent and powerful Juarez drug cartel.

The town had been without a police chief since this past May, when a band of 70 gunmen raided the town and murdered the previous chief, along with two of his officers as well as several civilians. After the attack, out of fear, the rest of the town's 20-officer police force resigned.

While the murder of a police chief by the hands of organized crime would be front-page news and cause for great alarm in the United States, high-profile murders of police officers and citizens alike by the powerful Mexican drug cartels have become commonplace.

On August 13, 2008, paramilitary gunmen wearing body armor, burst into a drug rehab center in Juarez. The attackers dragged several patients outside and executed them. At the time, a religious ceremony was taking place. Eight people, including a pastor were killed and six more were seriously wounded.

Those murders were among 43 which took place in Juarez over a three day period.

On June 4, 2008, husband and wife police officers Gabriel Padilla Perez and Claudia Tovar Carreon were shot to death in front of their

Juarez home, as they left for work. The couple left behind two small children. A day earlier, a 25-year-old pregnant woman was killed outside a shopping mall a few miles away, as a shootout broke-out between rival gang members.

In May of this year, the chief of Mexico's federal police force was assassinated entering his home in Mexico City. Commander Edgar Millan Gomez and his bodyguards were gunned down by several men in an ambush-style attack. He was shot nine times and died a short time later, after being taken to a hospital.

Commander Gomez was to date, the highest-ranking law enforcement official to fall victim to the current drug war. Many believe that his murder was in retaliation for the January arrest of Sinaloa Cartel leader Alfredo Beltran Leyva.

On April 26, 2008, 14 gang members were killed in a bloody shootout among rival cartel elements in the streets of Tijuana. The long-fought battle which took place in the middle of the night, was fought with high-powered rifles and machine guns.

There are four major drug cartels currently operating inside Mexico. The groups are extremely violent and have become very bold, regularly murdering police officers and various government officials. These cartels account for more than 80 percent of the illegal drugs sold in the United States, including marijuana, methamphetamine, cocaine, and heroin.

A list of the Mexican drug cartels follows:

Tijuana Cartel…Run by the Arellano Felix family. The cartel nearly collapsed in 2002, after Ramon Arellano Felix was killed by the police, and brother Benjamin was taken into custody. However, the cartel has since seen a resurgence in strength and violence of late, and continues to be a major player in the smuggling of marijuana and cocaine into the U.S.

Sinaloa Cartel…Infamous for the smuggling of cocaine from Columbia, and heroin from Southeast Asia. They also produce their own brand of heroin. U.S. law enforcement has identified Sinaloa Cartel distribution centers in Arizona, California, Texas, New York, and Chicago.

The Sinaloa Cartel uses the gangs known as MS-13 and the Mexican Mafia to distribute drugs inside the U.S.

Gulf Cartel…Utilizes an elite paramilitary group known as the Zetas as enforcers. Many of the Zetas were actually trained at

U.S. military bases, in an effort by this country to aid the Mexican government in their fight against the cartels. Upon their return to Mexico, they were recruited by the Gulf Cartel, who offered them a much higher salary than did the government.

The Zetas have proven to be ruthless fighters in the cartel's ongoing war with the Sinaloa Cartel.

The Gulf Cartel boasts of relationships with corrupt officials and is based in Matamoros, Tamaulipas. They also have major operations in the city of Nuevo Laredo and account for the increased violence now being seen there.

Juarez Cartel...Perhaps, the wealthiest of the cartels. According to the U.S. State Department, the Juarez Cartel "controls one of the primary transportation routes for billions of dollars worth of drug shipments entering the United States from Mexico annually."

The Juarez Cartel has been publicly posting hit lists containing the names of Juarez police officers. Many of those officers have been murdered, and still more have fled the city.

Kidnappings, torture, and shootouts have become a way of life in violence-plagued Juarez. That Mexican city which shares a border with El Paso, TX, has already seen an astounding 800 murders since January 2008.

In addition to the sale of narcotics, the cartels profit heavily by collecting so-called 'protection money' from legitimate businesses, street-level drug dealers, and those known as 'coyotes' who smuggle people illegally into the U.S. The cartels also regularly kidnap Mexicans as well as U.S. citizens for ransom, usually seeking a sum of about $300,000.Mexico's office of Public Security recently announced that since 2001, authorities have arrested 897 kidnappers. Incredibly, 56 of those arrested were actually public officials.

On August 25, 2008, a kidnapping ring was broken-up and the members taken into custody in the state of Nuevo Leon. The leader of the group was Comandante Sonia Virginia Bastida Morales. She is an agent in Mexico's AFI (that country's version of the FBI). At the time of her arrest, she and her two accomplices were holding two men for ransom.

The influence which the cartels are having on the people of Mexico is far-reaching and threatens every law-abiding person in that country. An example of this comes from a recent survey which reported that 120 of the 200 taxi drivers in the city of Chetumal, report to have been threatened with violence against their families, if they refused to deliver drugs on behalf of the local drug cartel.

An incredible example of how deeply corruption runs in Mexico came in 1997, when Mexican authorities seized a decommissioned U.S. Air Force C-130A which had been sold to the Mexican airline Aero Postal de Mexico. The plane was in fact being used to transport drugs from Central and South America. It was discovered that the owner of the airline had connections to the Tijuana Cartel.

A few facts on the violence being perpetrated by Mexico's drug cartels:

Since 2006, nearly 500 police officers, soldiers, and prosecutors have been killed by cartel gunmen.

According to the National Association of Former Border Patrol Officers, there have been more than 7,000 executions performed by Mexican drug cartels since December 1, 2006.

Cartels often behead their victims, and even release videos of taped executions on the internet.

The Zetas have been linked to several murders as far north as Dallas, TX.

According to the Department of Homeland Security, more than 3,000 families fled the city of Juarez in 2008, seeking refuge in the U.S.

In May 2008, Homeland Security officials announced to the press that there were at the time, three Mexican police chiefs seeking asylum in the U.S. Apparently, police officials have been seeking safety in the U.S. for more than a year.

Deputy Commissioner of Customs and Border Protection Jayson Ahern told the Associated Press: "They're basically abandoned by their police officers or police departments in many cases."

Ahern went on to say: "It's like a military fight. I don't think that generally the American public has any sense of the level of violence that occurs on the border."

On August 25, 2008, federal and local law enforcement officials told the Associated Press that Mexican drug cartels are now sending hit men into the U.S.

Officer Chris Mears of the El Paso Police Department told reporters: "We received credible information that drug cartels in Mexico have given permission to hit targets on the U.S. side of the border. One of the first things we did was to notify all officers in our department of the situation."

In July 2008, police in New Mexico and Texas received a cartel hit list, uncovered by U.S. Immigration and Customs Enforcement. The list contained the name of at least one New Mexico police officer.

Luna County Sheriff's Capt. Arturo Baeza told the press: "We have been concerned for quite some time that this thing will spill over here."

Of course, threats to U.S. law enforcement from drug smugglers is nothing new. Assaults on Border Patrol agents began rising at unprecedented rates a few years ago. Since 2001, assaults (which include shootings) have tripled, with 987 in 2007.

Snipers stay on the Mexican side of the border and move about freely. They fire a few shots at agents, then move to cover--only to fire again from another location. The tactics are typical of military sniper training. More than likely, the snipers are creating a diversion so that the smugglers can cross in another location. They know that the U.S. agents cannot pursue them into Mexico, and their own government is seemingly powerless to stop their activities.

In 2005, Border Patrol spokesman Andy Adame said: "We believe the vast majority of these assaults are directly tied to alien and drug smugglers based in Mexico."

Of course, Mexico's drug cartels are now operating within the interior of the U.S. According to the U.S. Department of Justice, the cartels now have operations in 231 U.S. cities. Atlanta, GA has been transformed into a major hub from which cartels methamphetamine is distributed throughout the east coast.

So far, Mexican President Felipe Calderon has deployed 45,000 troops nationwide to combat the cartels. However, the efforts by the Mexican government have done very little to stop the violence and the cartels appear to be winning.

With a largely unprotected border, and a Homeland Security chief who seems oblivious to the threat posed to American cities, it is very easy for cartel hit men to cross into the U.S.

If our elected representatives do not stop playing politics and find the courage to actually defend this nation's borders, it appears that we can expect to see the kind of violence now destroying Mexico in the streets of our own cities very soon.

Chapter 10

"United States Is Stupid"

"United States is stupid...I come back every time." Those words were spoken by Mexican national Rolando Mota-Campos to an immigration agent after his 11th arrest in the United States. Incredibly, Mota-Campos has been deported three times and has vowed to return again after completing his prison term and yet another undeniably meaningless deportation to Mexico.

Mota-Campos whose face is adorned with a teardrop tattoo, stood in a Norfolk, Va. federal courtroom in October 2007 to be sentenced for threatening to cut off a social worker's head with a machete.

U.S. District Judge Henry Coke Morgan Jr. said: "The defendant has expressly stated that he has no respect for the United States and that once deported he will re-enter again and come back to Newport News where his history of alcohol abuse will further endanger the residents of this district." Judge Morgan sentenced Mota-Campos to 14 1/2 years in prison.

While 43 year old Rolando Mota-Campos' personal reign of terror is apparently over at least for a few years, it is beyond sickening why this illegal alien with ties to the Mexican Mafia was able to disregard our border as well as the lives of innocent Americans for 19 years. He first entered this country illegally in 1988.

Mota-Campo's long criminal history in this country is as follows:

1992...abduction
1993...assault (2), DUI
1995...DUI, vehicular assault
1997...maiming, drunk in public

1998...attempted robbery
2003...DUI
2004...DUI, domestic violence (beating his wife and son)
2005...threatening to kill

The day after Mota-Campos was arrested with his 2004 DUI, he brutally attacked his wife and son. Fearing for her life, his wife then took their child and went into hiding. A few months later, he threatened to cut off the head of his wife's social worker with his machete because she would not tell him the whereabouts of his wife and child. Court documents reveal that Mota-Campos told her that "her sweet little head can come right off."

Though convicted numerous times on DUI charges, Mota-Campos has never served more than a 30-day sentence for that charge. Authorities point to the fact that he has used 16 different names as well as phony identification papers as the reason for the rather light punishment. This, despite his admission in 1993 to an immigration agent that he had killed someone while driving drunk in Mexico City.

Mota-Campos has entered this country illegally through the states of California, Arizona, and Texas.

This case is disgusting. However, it is certainly by no means unusual. The United States is filled with violent criminals who have entered this country illegally and who have no regard for human life.

On January 11, 2008, police arrested Mexican national Santana Batiz Aceves in Arizona and based on DNA evidence, charged him with 47 counts of rape. Police believe that Aceves is the notorious Chandler rapist, responsible for many child-rapes. The string of rapes began in 2006.

The 39 year old illegal alien had already been deported twice for drug charges in California. Aceves also faces charges of kidnapping, aggravated assault, sexual abuse of a minor, giving police false information, providing false documents, and trespassing.

Aceves was working as a heavy equipment operator and lived very close to two junior high schools.

These are but two of the many thousands of previously deported illegal aliens who have re-entered the United States, only to harm our citizens. They steal taxpayer services, they drive drunk on our highways, they kill our police officers, and they victimize our children.

Until the federal government actually gets serious about defending our border with Mexico, rather than actually encouraging the current invasion, it will continue to be open-season on American citizens. Perhaps, one day, we will be smart enough to elect a leader who will take their oath of office seriously, rather than another corrupt businessman who is willing to look the other way.

Chapter 11

Swine Flu Is Only The Latest Disease To Be Imported From Mexico

While all attention is on the current swine flu epidemic, dangerous diseases crossing into this country from Mexico, along with millions of illegal aliens is nothing new.

It is often said that the flood of illegal immigrants into this country is reaching 'epidemic proportions.' While that statement is true, it is just as true that the illegal immigrants pouring over the U.S./Mexican border are endangering this country with actual epidemics. Tuberculosis, hepatitis, dengue fever, chagas, and even leprosy are being imported into the U.S. inside the bodies of illegal aliens.

A virtual 'hot-zone' of disease can be found inside this nation's border states. Illegal immigrants have set up so-called "colonias" just inside the states of New Mexico, Texas, and Arizona. The shanty towns are comprised mostly of cardboard shacks and huts made with cast-off building materials. They have no sanitation, and are surrounded by mounds of garbage. The estimated 185,000 illegals share their makeshift towns with armies of rats. Of course, diseases only common to Central and South America run rampant in these places.

One of the imports to this country is chagas disease. It is caused by a parasite known as trypanosome. It is a blood-borne disease and is spread by triatomine insects. The parasite burrows into human tissue (usually in the face), where it then begins to multiply. In addition to being spread by insects, it can also be contracted through blood transfusions.

After cases of chagas were reportedly discovered to have been spread by transfusions in Canada, that nation began testing all blood donations for the disease.

Once thought to be nearly eradicated in this country, TB is now making a strong comeback. In a 2005 interview with Mother Jones Magazine, Dr. Reichman of The New Jersey TB Clinic said: "In the 1990's, cases among foreign born Americans rose from 29 percent to 41.6 percent. Antibiotic resistant strains from Mexico have migrated to Texas. Since three years ago, 16,000 new cases of TB were discovered in the United States. Half were foreign born. Strains of TB once only found in Mexico have migrated to the border states of Texas, Arizona, New Mexico, and California. It will move north as illegal aliens work in restaurants as cooks, dishwashers, and food handlers. We sit on the edge of a potential catastrophe."

In 2001, New York's Tuberculosis Control Program discovered that 81 percent of that city's new cases of TB were attributed to aliens.

Cases of TB are now being found in many areas of the country, where there are high concentrations of illegal aliens. In March of 2002, The Washington Post reported that Virginia's Prince William County experienced a 188 percent increase of TB infections over the previous year. Of course, the streets of Prince William County are over-run with illegal aliens seeking day-laborer jobs.

Less than two weeks ago, in Chicago, another outbreak of TB was feared, as an infected doctor possibly spread the virus throughout area hospitals. The unidentified physician worked at Evanston Hospital, Children's Memorial and Northwestern Memorial's Prentice Women's Hospital. Chicago has a "sanctuary" policy for illegal aliens, and consequently has a very large illegal population.

It costs between $250K to $1million to treat a patient with TB.

Despite the dangers presented by the swine flu and the fact that the World Health Organization has raised their threat level to 5 (out of 6), the U.S. government has refused to close our border to Mexico, where the flu has originated and where hundreds of deaths have occurred.

During an April 27 press conference, DHS Janet Napolitano said: "Well, as I said yesterday, we're already doing passive surveillance at the border. And with respect to closing the border, again, you would close the border if you thought you could contain disease, the spread of disease. But the disease already is in a number of states within the United States, so the containment issue doesn't really play out. This particular flu, you can actually have it for a couple of days before you show any symptoms, and so even if—people could be coming through now, even under passive surveillance, who actually have the flu. So that's a very difficult judgment to make."

Then on NBC's Today Show Napolitano gave the real reason behind this administration's unwillingness to close the border.

Napolitano told viewers: "You have to look at what the costs of that are. We literally have thousands of trucks and lots of commerce that cross that border. We have food products and other things that go across that border. So that would be a very, very heavy cost."

So, we cannot protect ourseves from the dangerous virus because of "Commerce!"

As usual, business interest are put ahead of the safety and health of the American public. Fears are growing that as this virus continues to ravage Mexico, scores of people will flood into this country, over our largely unprotected border. Of course, many of them will arrive already infected.

It seems that every nation except the United States is taking this outbreak seriously. Take a look at the following headlines from around the world:

"Swine flu prompts EU warning on travel to U.S."

" British holiday companies suspend flights to Mexico"

" Air Canada and Westjet are suspending flights and vacation tours to Mexico"

" Argentina suspends flights from Mexico"

" Cuba halts flights to Mexico as flu virus spreads"

" Cruise lines cancel Mexico stops over flu fear "

The threats posed to our country by illegal immigration are many. However, our political leaders will undoubtedly continue to ignore them. Our own president is willing to place all Americans at risk, in exchange for securing the Latino vote for the Democratic Party.

If left unchecked, illegal immigration will destroy this nation one way or another.

Chapter 12

The Death Toll Will Continue To Mount As Long As The Border Remains Unsecured

With the 2009 arrest of a Salvadoran national for the murder of intern Chandra Levy who went missing in 2001, the issue of crime attributed to illegal aliens is and should be on the minds of millions of Americans.

At the time of his arrest, Ingmar Guandique who was is in this country illegally, was already in prison for the assault of two other women in Washington D.C. He was actually arrested only a few days after Levy's disappearance on burglary charges. Though law enforcement was aware of his illegal status, Immigration and Customs Enforcement was not notified due to the District's sanctuary policy.

While Chandra Levy may be the most well known American who has been killed by an illegal alien, she is only one in a staggeringly large and ever-growing group.

The federal government does not keep comprehensive statistics on the number of crimes committed in this country by illegal aliens. Taking a look at the results of a few independent studies, it is not surprising that they don't.

In 2006, Rep. Steve King (R-Iowa) released the results of a study which found that 4,380 Americans are murdered every year by illegal aliens. The study also concluded that 4,745 Americans are killed every year by illegal aliens driving drunk.

In 2005, the Government Accountability Office announced the results of a study which examined the criminal history of 55,322 illegal aliens who were incarcerated in federal, state, and local institutions during the year 2003. The results of that study follow:

The 55,322 illegal aliens in the study accounted for a total of 459,614 arrests (or eight arrests per illegal alien). Their arrests represented a total of nearly 700,000 criminal offenses (or 13 offenses per illegal alien). 36 percent of those studied had been arrested at least five times previously.

Peter Wagner, the author of "The Dark Side of Illegal Immigration," summed up the situation when he told WorldNetDaily: "While the vast majority of illegal aliens are decent people who work hard and are only trying to make a better life for themselves and their families, it is also a fact that a disproportionately high percentage of illegal aliens are criminals and sexual predators. That is part of the dark side of illegal immigration and when we allow the 'good' in we get the 'bad' along with them. The question is, how much 'bad' is acceptable and at what price?"

Speaking of the price we are paying, the Ohio Jobs and Justice Political Action Committee has set up an on-line memorial for victims who were killed by illegal aliens. They continuously update the site and have an extensive list of victims' names, along with some information on the victim, as well as a brief history on the criminal case. What follows is a small sampling of some of the more recent cases:

Victim: Breanna Slaughter-Eck
Age: 12
In late 2008, Breanna was riding her bicycle in San Jose, California when she was allegedly hit and killed by unlicensed illegal alien Adriana Fierro DeMarin, who now sits in jail awaiting trial.

Victim: Nayashieka Cooper
Age: 19
Ms. Cooper and her 3 year old son were walking down a street in Athens, GA, when Mexican national Abel Gonzalez-Perez ran her over and immediately fled the scene (police captured him three days later). Her little boy sat by his mother and watched helplessly as she lay dying next to him.

In January 2009, Gonzalez-Perez pled guilty to DUI, vehicular manslaughter, and hit and run.

Victim: Lila Meizel
Age: 83
Ramon Alvarado, Jose Alvarado, and Ana Rodas are all in the country illegally and have been arrested for the 2008 murder of Mrs. Meizel. The three allegedly beat the elderly woman to death, then burned her body in an attempt to cover-up the crime scene.
Even though the Alvarado cousins had several prior arrests, local authorities never notified ICE of their immigration status because Montgomery County, MD has a sanctuary policy in place.

Victim: Dean Knospe
Age: 71
On January 22, 2009, Mexican national Eulalio Haro was convicted in the 2006 hit and run death of Mr. Knospe. Haro who was driving under the influence, hit Knospe who was riding his motorcycle, and drove away, leaving him to die on the road.
Haro had been previously deported after serving a prison sentence for another crash in 1993, but re-entered the country illegally.

Victim: William Sullo III
Age: 30
In November 2008, Ecuadorian national Jose Maldanado Luzuriaga was arrested for the murder of Mr. Sullo. Police allege that he killed Mr. Sullo who worked as a bartender at the Salute Restaurant in Philadelphia, PA, because he refused to serve him anymore alcohol and later had him removed from the bar.
Luzuriaga allegedly waited outside the bar for Sullo to leave, and upon seeing the bartender exit the building, rammed his F-150 pickup truck into him. He has been charged with criminal homicide, attempted homicide (he nearly ran over another bartender in the parking lot), reckless endangerment, and not possessing a driver's license.

Luzuriaga told police that he had been living in the U.S. for five years.
The on-line memorial goes on and on with names of Americans both young and old who have been sacrificed for political reasons.

Not Congress nor our former or current President will actually defend our border, and stop the flow of illegal immigration into the United States.

For many years, the Republicans wanted to keep the border open to fill the country with cheap labor, which benefits business owners by undercutting wages for everyone. The Democrats have sought to keep the border unprotected to bring in millions of potential new voters, which is why that party pays so much lip service to the plight of illegal aliens.

Whether they seek those willing to work for sub-standard wages, or voters who will keep them in power, it is the American people who have been sold out by both parties.

Every time I learn that a family has been attacked, or a child has been killed by an illegal alien, I think this must be the tipping point. There are certain dates in this ongoing tragedy which stand out more than others:

Such as on June 22, 2008, when three members of the Bologna family were gunned down by Salvadoran national and MS-13 gang member Edwin Ramos. Tony Bologna, 48, and his sons Michael, 20, and Matthew, 16 were shot to death by Ramos with an AK-47 as they sat in their car on a crowded street, in the city's Excelsior District.

Or on September 10, 2008, the day the parents of 3-year-old Marten Kudlis buried their son at Fairmount Cemetery, who was killed while waiting for his ice cream in a Denver Baskin and Robbins.

Guatemalan national Francis Hernandez slammed into a pickup truck, which was then pushed into the ice cream shop's window. The toddler was sitting at a table in front of that window, and was sent flying as the truck came crashing through it.

This nation sits on the brink of an economic meltdown, while our cities are becoming hunting grounds for predatory criminals. We have enough problems in this country without importing them from foreign lands.

Because we live with it everyday, most Americans understand and fear this growing threat. However, our elected representatives continue to turn a blind eye and a deaf ear to the mounting death toll.

A weary nation must ask the question…How many Americans have to die before the border is secured?

Chapter 13

Those Who Hire Illegal Aliens Are Today's Slave Masters

Africans were brought to this country against their will, thus breaking the laws of God. Mexicans are smuggled into this country illegally, thus breaking the laws of man. The former as well as the latter have been brought here for the purposes of cheap labor. While the issue of slavery nearly destroyed this nation during the 19th century, today's slave trade is also wreaking havoc upon the Republic.

The 'plantation mentality' is alive and well throughout this country's businesses which rely upon a non-skilled labor force. Industries such as agriculture, landscaping, hospitality, and construction have filled their ranks with illegal aliens.

In most cases, these illegal workers are paid less than even the Federal Minimum Wage. In some cases, they are actually paid nothing. Unscrupulous employers exploit illegal aliens for huge profits. The illegal worker is always fearful of detection, therefore he cannot make complaints of inhuman working conditions nor of labor violations. Unlike any American citizen, the illegal alien worker has no legal recourse against unethical employers.

Often times, employers who frequently hire illegal aliens will place a dozen or more of their workers into a tiny sub-standard house or apartment (which the employer either rents in his name or owns). Every morning, a company truck arrives to transport them to the job site, and brings them home in the evening. On payday, many of those same employers deduct the costs of housing and transportation from their workers' pay.

Eager to make any amount of U.S. dollars and constantly aware of his illegal status in this country, he simply accepts the mere pittance afforded him and keeps his mouth shut.

For years, we have heard American businessmen complain that Americans no longer want jobs which require hard physical labor. Those same businessmen then tell us that Mexican men will perform these jobs, therefore our economy is dependent upon the use of illegal aliens. Prior to this nation's Civil War, Southern plantation owners were offering much the same excuse as to why it was necessary to import and enslave Africans.

Regardless of which party is in control, the federal government will continue to turn a blind eye to the problem of illegal immigration. Of course, many American businessmen who hire illegal aliens, contribute a great deal of money to candidates from both the Republican and Democratic parties. As far as the leadership of either party is concerned, there is no problem.

Just as waves of humanity daily cross our border in search of low-paying jobs--higher-paying American jobs are flowing overseas. The failure of our political leaders to retard either of those national crises, is breaking the collective back of the American worker. Our politicians are much more concerned with lining their own pockets, than they are with the plight of hard-working Americans.

Our criminal politicians have entered into a partnership with criminal businessmen. Large amounts of money, stemming from the tremendous profits made on the backs of illegal aliens are being funneled into both parties. Call it a donation, call it a bribe, the result is the same--the interests of American citizens are being ignored and our laws are being trampled upon.

Nearly 145 years ago, the federal government ended slavery in this country, sacrificing over 600,000 American lives to do so. Today however, the federal government is in business with the slave masters. Who will end this atrocity, defend our border, and restore American sovereignty?

We the people must find a way to protect our borders and restore order. We must dispense with political leaders who refuse to uphold the law and defend this nation. It is becoming painfully clear that we need a new political party, one which will enforce the laws, and place the interests of American families before those of multi-national corporations.

Chapter 14

Years Of Extending Loans To Illegal Aliens Have Helped Crash The Economy

After writing several articles about this country's mortgage meltdown and the little-talked about role which illegal aliens have played in this crisis, a woman who I will call "Mary" contacted me with inside information on the crisis. What follows is a brief interview I conducted with Mary. (I am protecting her identity because she still works in the mortgage business.)

Q) What is your background and who have you worked for?

A) I am in the Mortgage Industry and personally audited thousands of sub prime loans while working as a contractor. The last company I worked for was EMC, previously owned by Bear Stearns so I thought I would share the caveat on these loans.

Q) When my wife and I bought our home, we had to provide a mountain of documentation, including federal tax returns. How have the mortgage lenders allowed illegal aliens to enter into a mortgage loan without the proper documents?

A) The Sub Prime underwriting guidelines had special requirements for, what was called, Foreign Nationals....30% down and full credit package including credit references from their country of origin and a valid Visa. To circumvent this requirement, the applications were marked that the borrower was a US citizen then, regardless if the credit profile did not support such a claim, an underwriter was not allowed to question. This along with use of stolen SS# or use of their American born child's SS# and lax credit requirements that allowed alternative credit, helped cover the ruse. All required documentation was fraudulent and with the large use of a/k/a's, information was hard to track.

Q) What did management do when it was discovered that a stolen Social Security number was being used by a borrower?

A) It was not uncommon to find a SS# being used by up to 23 other people or a borrower with 27 a/k/a's. Management would often clear a loan that you tagged as fraudulent so it wouldn't be shelved.

Q) What was the worst case you have seen?

A) One borrower stole the SS# of a retiree and took out $3.5 million in loans, turned around and did cash-out refi's, then fled the country. The retiree was left with ruined credit, $3.5 million in loans and trouble with the IRS. Over 50% of the sub primes were for cash-out refi's. Regardless of the loan criteria used to pull random samplings for audits, the majority of the last names were Hispanic. The loans I audited were primarily in CA, NV, AZ, FL, CO, compare those to the states with the highest number of foreclosures & illegal aliens.

Q) What is your opinion on the $750 billion bailout engineered by former Treasurer Hank Paulson and approved by Congress?

A) During the bailout, I called my Congressman and other leadership including Barney Frank and asked if there was a provision within the Bill that prohibited illegal aliens from being bailed-out.....the answer was no. I asked if there was a provision in the Bill that helped homeowners that did not take out sub primes but are faced with losing their home due to the negative impact of sub primes and was told..... no. So in other words, those that committed crimes to obtain the loans will get a helping hand to bail them out, compliments of the US Taxpayer!

Q) Any final thoughts?

A) I cannot tell you how angry I am over this and you are right.....
Congress will not talk about it. I have written to mine [Congressman]
several times over the last year, yet my only response is their standard
form letter. When I call and demand an answer, I have been told
someone will get back with me, of course that never happens. Looks
like we are picking up where we left off before the bail-out.

If Mary's observations did not anger you, I am certain that the
next bit of information will do the trick.

Of course, we all know that, on October 26, 2001, President Bush
signed the USA Patriot Act. However, I would wager to say that almost
no one knows that contained in section 326(b) of the USA Patriot
Act is a provision that allows US banks to accept Mexican Matricula
Consular cards as a valid form of ID for opening bank accounts.

It should be noted that while our President and Congress ordered
American banks to recognize these Mexican-issued cards, there is not
one Mexican bank which accepts their own government's Matricula
Consular card as a valid form of ID, because the bearer's identity is
basically untraceable.

The following is a list of U.S. banks (both regional and national)
and mortgage insurers which are known to offer home loan programs
targeted at illegal aliens:

-Bank of America
-Citigroup
-Deutsche Bank AG
-Fifth Third Bancorp
-Genworth Financial Inc.
-J.P. Morgan Chase
-Liberty Financial
-Mortgage Guarantee Insurance Corp.
-Plaza Bank
-Wachovia
-Wells Fargo

So there you have it. Those elected to represent we the American people, decided instead to represent the bankers and allow illegal aliens to borrow money, often using the stolen Social Security numbers of American citizens. This so-called sub-prime mortgage crisis was actually a crisis of massive fraud.

And why not?...The banks who made the loans have lost nothing, because the taxpayers have been forced to bail them out for their risky and even illegal loans.

Chapter 15

Why The Catholic Church Encourages Illegal Immigration

As countless child sex abuse scandals have rocked the Catholic Church over the last several years, American families have been leaving the church in droves. As American men and women whisk away their children from the potential risk of molestation in the Catholic church, they also take their much needed money. The coffers of U.S. Catholic churches have been running on empty and the church sees the pocketbooks of illegal immigrants as its only hope.

During Pope Benedict XVI's 2008 visit to the United States, he gave many speeches and sermons. Among other things, the Pope admonished Americans to adopt a welcoming attitude toward those who break our laws by entering this country illegally. Benedict said: "I want to encourage you and your communities to continue to welcome the immigrants who join your ranks today, to share their joys and hopes, to support them in their sorrows and trials and to help them flourish in their new home.

It was discovered that the Pontifical Commission for Latin America, a Vatican-based group which answers directly to the Pope has made a large donation to help build a shelter for Central Americans on their illegal journey to the United States. The money was given to the Brothers On The Path refuge, located in the Mexican city of Ixtepec.

Between 2005-2007, the number of Central American nationals caught by the Border Patrol entering the U.S. illegally has averaged 11 percent of their total apprehensions. While the majority of the 875,000 caught sneaking across the border annually are Mexicans, those coming from countries such as Guatemala, Honduras, and El Salvador are adding to the incredible burden placed on our Border Patrol agents.

Along with the usual problems posed by illegal immigration, a particularly violent gang known as MS-13 hails from El Salvador, but now has many Honduran and Guatemalan members as well. In addition to other parts of the country, MS-13 has been gaining a large presence in Northern Virginia, and is responsible for several machete attacks in the area. In 2005, an Alexandria teenager lost four fingers during a savage encounter with MS-13 members and a Fairfax man also became a victim of a MS-13 machete attack.

In June 2005, Los Angeles Cardinal Roger Mahony wrote an op-ed piece for the Los Angeles Times in which he defended and even encouraged illegal aliens to enter this country. Of course, Mexicans and other Latin Americans are overwhelmingly devout Catholics. Mahony along with the rest of the church's hierarchy is undoubtedly anxious to tap this potential source of income.

In 2006, Cardinal Mahony directed all priests in his 288 parish archdiocese to simply ignore any federal law which requires anyone working on behalf of the church to inquire into the citizenship of anyone seeking help (The Catholic church offers assistance to illegal aliens applying for various welfare programs). The directive was given by Mahony in response to the immigration bill passed by the U.S. House of Representatives in December 2005, which declared all illegal aliens "criminals" and mandated the prosecution to anyone who knowingly aided an illegal alien.

For decades, the Catholic Church shielded and protected child-molesting priests. As complaints would come pouring-in from parents threatening to involve the police, the church would simply ship the offending priest off on a sabbatical, eventually pawning them off on another unsuspecting parish where the process would begin again. That practice is nothing more than aiding and abetting known criminals. The enormous toll of lives destroyed by this disgusting and cowardly exercise by the Catholic Church will never be fully known.

The Catholic Church has been forced to pay-out millions to the victims of pedophile priests. Fed up with the hypocrisy and disregard for the lives of innocent children, many Americans have fled the Church. In the Boston Archdiocese alone, 65 churches have been forced to close their doors due to a sharp decline in parishioners.

Boston was once considered the center of the American Catholic society. Catholic worshipers in that city were shocked to learn of the outrageous behavior displayed by Cardinal Bernard Law and the offending priests he protected for so many years. One priest that Law moved around to several different parishes was Father Paul Shanley. As it turned out, Fr. Shanley was not only a molester, but an advocate for NAMBLA (North American Man-Boy Love Association). While Shanley was eventually convicted of child rape, Cardinal Law was rewarded by Pope John Paul II, who brought him to Rome where he now holds a prominent position within the Vatican.

For many American Catholics, it became obvious that their church would never take seriously the issue of children being victimized by child-raping priests. It also became obvious that the church would never take true responsibility for the role the leaders of the church played in harboring these monsters. It is little wonder that so many now well-informed American Catholics refuse to ever return their children as well as their donations to the church.

The illegal aliens represent exactly what the Catholic Church needs right now...largely uneducated and devoted worshipers with jobs. The illegal aliens will be all-too happy to place their children in Catholic schools (largely funded by school vouchers). If Congress ever grants amnesty to all illegal immigrants, they will fill the now-darkened parishes throughout the U.S.

Most of these people speak very little English and most lack even an elementary school education, they are much more likely to keep their mouths shut once the priests begin to have their way with their children. The shell game of shifting molesting priests around will begin again and the faithful will continue to fork-over ten percent of their wages to the church.

The Catholic Church has also helped to organize the massive illegal alien rallies seen in recent years around the nation. The March 2006 rally held in Washington, D.C. was sponsored by among others the Archdiocese of Washington's Office of Justice and Service, Catholic Charities of the Arlington Diocese, and the Catholic Social Justice Lobby Network. Baltimore churches St. Michael and St. Patrick even sent a four bus convoy filled with illegal aliens to the Washington rally.

A high-ranking official with the Diocese of Arlington, Va. named Father Jose Hoyos played to the crowd when he said: "I want to pray for all the representatives and the senators and the president of the United States, because if they were Christians they would not pass this kind of law."

According to the Catholic Church, it is now somehow un-Christian to protect the sovereignty of one's own nation.

The aid and encouragement given to illegal aliens has angered many people who still care about preserving the Republic and maintaining it as a nation of laws. Al Garza, executive director of the Minuteman Civil Defense Corps recently said: "It's not only provocative, it's sinful. What they're really doing is saying, 'Look, even though the United States has laws, we're going to help you break the laws to realize your dream.' "

In the 1940's, the Catholic Church helped Nazis escape prosecution to begin new lives in South America. At least from the 1960's to the present, the church chose to protect child-molesting priests over innocent children. Now, to save itself, that same Catholic Church is encouraging an illegal invasion of this country...Is it any wonder that this church has become irrelevant to most Americans?

Chapter 16

Branding Americans As "Racists" To Further Their Agenda

In 2007, former Bush nominee and columnist Linda Chavez published an article in which she accuses Americans who stand in opposition to the Bush-McCain-Kennedy Amnesty Bill as racists. Alleging racism is the favorite tactic being used by the pro-amnesty crowd. It is often used by those who find themselves on the wrong side of the argument.

Let us refresh our memory...In 2001, Linda Chavez was nominated by President Bush for the Secretary of Labor position. Her nomination fell apart when it was discovered that she had long-employed an illegal alien as a housekeeper. In her ensuing unofficial role, she often acted as a cheerleader for Bush and his desire to turn the U.S. into Mexico.

Townhall.com published the article by Linda Chavez in which she attacked the American people, or at least the ones who value U.S. sovereignty. In her essay entitled "Latino Fear and Loathing," she repeatedly refers to those of us who oppose the amnesty legislation as "xenophobes."

Chavez said: "We need to quit pretending that the "No Amnesty" crowd is anything other than what it is: a tiny group of angry, frightened and prejudiced loudmouths backed by political opportunists who exploit them."

Apparently, Chavez believes that 80 percent of the American public is a tiny group! However, she is right that we are angry and frightened. We are angry that foreign nationals who have invaded our country will now be rewarded for their transgressions. We are frightened at the possibility of adding between 40-100 million mostly illiterate new immigrants to this country, over the next 20 years. We may be prejudiced in that we prefer the American way of life as opposed to a Third World existence.

Chavez went on to wrongly compare this nation's ever-growing illegal alien population with the European immigrants who came to America's shores in the early 1900's. She wrote: 'What is said today of the Mexicans, Guatemalans, Salvadorans and others was once said of Germans, Swedes, the Irish, Italians, Poles, Jews, and others. The only difference is that in the past the xenophobes could speak freely, unconstrained by a veneer of political correctness."

Chavez simply trotted-out the same old tired argument that all immigrants are alike. While it is true that many immigrants face hardships and prejudice, that is where the comparison ends. The massive waves of European immigrants came here legally and most made assimilation a priority. The illegal aliens now entering this country from Mexico, and Central America are not observing our laws and make very little effort to even learn English.

While those European immigrants humbly waved American flags as they lined the streets of New York on July 4th, the illegal aliens defiantly wave Mexican flags on our streets as they demand their 'rights.' To compare the European immigrants of the early 20th century to the current lawless invaders, is an affront to the families of everyone who has legally immigrated to the United States.

Here are a few facts that Linda Chavez left out of her article:

-In 2005, over 380,000 anchor babies were born in the U.S. No less than 97 percent of the hospital delivery costs were paid by the American public.

-According to the Federation for American Immigration Reform, illegal aliens receive $43.7 billion annually in Medicaid and Medicare benefits.

-42 percent of students in California public schools do not speak English.

-K-12 expenses for illegal aliens cost U.S. taxpayers $7.4 billion annually.

-Over half of Los Angeles area gang members are illegal aliens.

-Over 9,000 Americans (homicides & DUI's) are murdered annually by illegal aliens.

-29 percent (630,000) of this country's prison population is comprised of illegal aliens. This currently costs the American public $1.6 billion annually.

Illegal immigration costs American taxpayers $346 billion annually.

Chapter 17

Like Many in Power, Sen. John McCain's Loyalty Does Not Lie With The United States

During his failed 2008 campaign, John McCain once again proved his contempt for the American people as well as his disregard for U.S. sovereignty. McCain chose a Mexican conman to fill a top campaign position.

McCain appointed Juan Hernandez as his so-called 'Hispanic outreach director.' Hernandez was born in Fort Worth, TX to a Mexican father and an American mother. He served as the director of the Presidential Office of Mexicans Living Abroad under Vicente Fox. He holds dual U.S./Mexican citizenship and was the first U.S. born person to serve as a cabinet member of the Mexican government.

Many of you have probably seen Hernandez during one of his many appearances on MSNBC, CNN, or Fox News. Anytime the illegal immigration debate heats up, Hernandez begins making the talk show rounds. Looking not unlike a Mexican bandito, he sits in front of the cameras extolling the virtues of the Mexican invaders, while soft-selling the negative impact they have on this country.

Hernandez has worked for years lobbying U.S. governors to issue drivers' licenses to illegal aliens living in their respective states. While in his official role for the Mexican government, he pressured Western Union to lower or drop altogether their fees for wire transfers for illegal aliens sending money back home to Mexico.

Hernandez is an ardent supporter of the re-conquest by Mexico of the American Southwest, and hosted lectures on the subject at the Center for U.S.-Mexico Studies in Dallas which he founded in 1995. He once told Congressman Tom Tancredo (R-CO) that the North American Southwest "is not two countries, it's just a region."

Here are a few interesting quotes from John McCain's friend:

"I never knew the border as a limitation; I'd be delighted if all of us could come and go between these two marvelous countries."

"We have recognized that the Mexican population is 100 million in Mexico and 23 million who live in the United States...We are a united nation."

Mexican immigrants "are going to keep one foot in Mexico and are not going to assimilate."

"We are betting that the Mexican population in the United States ...will think Mexico first."

However, we should not be surprised that John McCain would be so closely associated with someone who advocates the invasion of the United States by Mexican nationals. After all, McCain himself has spent many hours working on behalf of those same invaders.

After the massive illegal alien protests of 2006, McCain made the following statement; "If such demonstrations continue, I think we will have a bill for the President to sign soon. The more debate, the more demonstrations, the more likely we will prevail."

Under McCain's immigration bill, even members of Mexican drug gangs would have received amnesty by simply signing a statement in which they renounced their gang affiliation; the so-called 'background checks' that illegal aliens would have received were only of the 24-hour variety, which reveal very little if anything, and would have then been given a six month worker card. Immigration and Customs Enforcement agents would have traveled the country handing-out amnesty applications to suspected illegal aliens (Not kidding!), and all immigration enforcement would have ended.

All this from the man who at the 2008 Republican National Convention, told us to "Stand up for America!"

Chapter 18

The Consequences Of 'Sanctuary' Policies

On October 22, 2008, the First District Court of Appeals for the State of California ruled that the San Francisco Police must follow state law which requires police officers to contact federal authorities when they arrest anyone for a narcotics violation, when they suspect the person to be either a legal or illegal alien.

The appellate court ruling has reversed a lower court decision which claimed that San Francisco police officers were not required to comply with California state law, when arresting someone they suspected to be a foreign national.

The group Judicial Watch filed the lawsuit against San Francisco Police Chief Heather Fong, on behalf of San Francisco resident Charles Fonseca.

Shortly after the ruling, Judicial Watch President Tom Fitton said: "This landmark ruling strikes at the heart of the sanctuary movement for illegal aliens. San Francisco and other sanctuary cities are not above the law. This court ruling exposes the lie behind the argument that state and local law enforcement cannot help enforce immigration laws."

The particular law in question, which provided the basis for the lawsuit follows:

Section 11369 of the Health and Safety Code (Section 11369) states: "When there is reason to believe that any person arrested for a violation [of any of 14 specified drug offenses] may not be a citizen of the United States, the arresting agency shall notify the appropriate agency of the United States having charge of deportation matters."

This ruling will now force San Francisco's police chief to become compliant with state law and direct her officers to report all suspects whose immigration status is in question, when that suspect is arrested for drug violations. Given the fact that 90 percent of the illegal drugs sold in this country are brought in from Mexico, this ruling promises to be very effective in dealing with Latin American drug gangs, now responsible for a great deal of violence in California and beyond..

In San Francisco, on June 22, 2008, three members of the Bologna family were gunned down by Salvadoran national and gang member Edwin Ramos. Tony Bologna, 48, and his sons Michael, 20, and Matthew, 16 were shot to death by Ramos as they sat in their car on a crowded street, in the city's Excelsior District.

Ramos who is a member of the notoriously violent drug gang known as MS-13, shot the Bologna family to death because Tony Bologna had temporarily blocked the car in which Ramos was traveling, as the two cars made their way through an intersection. The Bologna men were returning home from a family barbecue.

As a juvenile, Ramos had committed felony attempted robbery and assault.

Shortly after the shooting, the San Francisco Chronicle reported, Juvenile Probation Department officials, did not report Ramos to federal immigration authorities for possible deportation because of San Francisco's stated sanctuary policy.

The devastated wife and mother Danielle Bologna is now suing the city of San Francisco over the sanctuary policy , which contributed to the death of her family.

This ruling comes too late to have saved the lives of the Bologna family, as well as thousands of other Americans who have lost their lives at the hands of illegal aliens. However, it is a positive step in forcing those sworn to "protect and serve" to actually do that for American citizens, and stop protecting those who enter this country only to victimize our citizens.

Chapter 19

Stop Illegal Immigration and the 'Healthcare Crisis' Will End

With the heated debate over government health care reform raging, while our insurance premiums and co-pays are rapidly rising, the number one culprit behind out-of-control health care costs is being ignored. Along with a host of other crimes, illegal aliens are stealing health care for which the rest of us must pay.

The enormous bills which illegal aliens leave unpaid at American hospitals, leave those hospitals with two choices: They can either distribute those costs among their paying customers, or operate annually at a loss and eventually close their doors.

In 2003, the American Southwest saw 77 hospitals enter bankruptcy due to unpaid medical bills incurred by illegal aliens. Over the last several years, a staggering 84 hospitals in California alone have been forced out of business due to the growing crisis. Hospitals which manage to remain open, pass the unpaid costs onto the rest of us, which translates into more out-of-pocket expenses and higher insurance premiums for Americans.

Everyday, pregnant Mexican and Central American women on the verge of giving birth, make their way across the U.S. border to have their baby in an American hospital. These children become infamous "Anchor Babies" so prized by their criminal parents. Once the child is born on American soil, he or she instantly attains U.S. citizenship. Not only are the parents almost always allowed to stay, but since they have no income, the baby is eligible for welfare, WIC, Food Stamps, etc.-- all at the expense of the great American taxpayer.

At one of North Carolina's Goshen Medical Centers, nursing assistant Jessica Roberts told USAToday in 2008, about an illegal alien who arrived more than eight months pregnant with her eighth child!

There are 350,000 of these so-called Anchor Babies born in the U.S. every year. It is estimated that they consume $118 billion annually in government services.

A 2007 March of Dimes survey placed the average cost of an uncomplicated, vaginal birth in a U.S. hospital at $8,800, with the average cost of a cesarean birth at $11,000.

Of course, these hospitals have no choice but to treat these women along with their newborn babies. However, the bills racked-up in the process always go unpaid.

According to a 2000 report by the United States/Mexico Border Counties Coalition, counties along the Mexican border lost over $800 million in health care services, at least 25% of that could be attributed to unpaid bills incurred by illegal aliens.

The American border states currently shoulder the brunt of the burden, for instance the Texas state comptroller estimates illegal aliens cost hospitals $1.3 billion in 2006 alone.

In California, a 2004 study conducted by FAIR (the Federation for American Immigration Reform) placed the now bankrupt state's annual cost for treating illegal aliens at $1.4 billion.

But with the spread of illegal immigration now throughout the U.S., the same such studies in 2005 found that health care costs for illegal aliens in Colorado and Minnesota were $31 million and $17 million, respectively.

In recent years, North Carolina has seen an explosion in the state's illegal alien population, as well as sky-rocketing medical costs. According to a University of North Carolina study, one in four new residents to the state from 1990 to 2004 was an illegal alien. The Pew Hispanic Center claims there are now more than 300,000 illegal aliens living in North Carolina.

In 2008, Jeff Spade, vice president of the North Carolina Hospital Association told USAToday: "It's exploded the amount for hospitals, the burden of the uninsured immigrant is huge. It's exploded the amount of work that they have to do."

A March 2007 article in the Journal of the American Medical Association claimed that during the period 2001-2004, emergency Medicaid costs for illegal aliens rose by 28% in North Carolina.

Duplin General Hospital in Kanansville, NC, now faces a rather bleak financial future due to the large influx of illegal aliens, and their unpaid medical bills. CEO Harvey Case recently addressed the hospital's lack of profits, when he said: "We're living off reserves."

U.S. hospitals often seek help for the unpaid bills as well as with transportation back to Mexico from the Mexican Consulate offices. However, the Mexican government rarely even arranges flights for their severely injured citizens to return home.

The illegal alien patient usually ends up staying in the hospital for weeks or months, with the hospital usually paying for a flight home, along with the enormous unpaid bill.

A 2008 New York Times article told the incredible story of a 1999 Florida car crash which left Guatemalan national Luis Alberto Jimenez with severe and permanent physical and mental injuries. After spending more than $1 million on Jimenez's treatment, and failed attempts to secure assistance from the government of Guatemala, the Florida hospital eventually paid to fly Jimenez back to his own country.

The incredible part of the story…Jimenez is now suing the Florida hospital, which he now says "falsely imprisoned" him and deported him against his will, to avoid anymore unpaid medical bills.

We have been told by our government that the number of illegal aliens currently inside the U.S. is about 12 million. However, we have been given this same figure for the last seven years, and even then that figure was considered very low by those who have studied the problem of illegal immigration.

With close to one million crossing our border with Mexico illegally every year, the number of course, is much higher than 12 million. Just like American citizens, illegal aliens get sick, they get injured, and they give birth. However, unlike most Americans, illegal aliens do not pay any portion of their medical bills. Many use fake or stolen Social Security numbers, as well as aliases and move back and forth across our unprotected border without detection.

Of course, we know that nothing in life is free, someone has to pay for it. Hospitals are not the federal government, therefore they cannot simply print money out of thin air to cover their expenses. So, all of the bills left unpaid by this country's illegal aliens are being paid by all of us who pay for our own healthcare, as well as through our federal and state income taxes.

Though President Obama will never mention this hard truth, if we simply ordered all illegal aliens out of the country and deported the ones who refused the order, as well as place our military along the border...Healthcare costs would stop rising and could even drop.

We do not need a government takeover of the best healthcare system in the world, nor do we need an amnesty bill for illegal aliens (a.k.a Comprehensive Immigration Reform), we only need to defend our border and expel those here illegally.

It's really very simple...Put an end to illegal immigration, and you put an end to the 'healthcare crisis.'

Chapter 20

'Raza Studies'...Teaching Racism in Our Classrooms

In recent years, there has been an investigation into what "Raza Studies" (also known as Mexican-American Studies) is teaching in their classes. Quotes in their books such as, "Kill the gringos" and teaching the children about 3 Plans they have had to throw the "gringos" back to Europe and take over the Southwest (now many want the entire U.S. as they have had so much success infiltrating all 50 states with thousands to millions of Mexicans in cities and states around the U.S.).

One quote in one of their books states, "The supporters (of the Plan of San Diego – one of the 3 Plans) would execute all white males over age 16..." (pg. 167 of "Occupied America" by Rodolfo Acuna, 5th edition, copyright 2004, Pearson/Longman). In this book, they refer to white people as "rednecks", "WASPS", "gabachos" (a derogatory term in Spanish), "gringos", etc., etc. Other books used to teach the children are written by Communists, Socialists, and other radicals. Mexicans refer to themselves as "La Raza" (The Race) as if they are the only Race. And they teach "racism".

Their motto is "Por La Raza – todo; fuera de La Raza – nada!" (Translation: For The (Mexican) Race – everything; (anyone) outside The (Mexican) Race (gets) nothing!" They even have a so-called "social club" in our schools called M.E.C.H.A. (which stands for Chicano Student Movement for Aztlan) which is based on "The Spiritual Plan of Aztlan" (one of the aforementioned 3 Plans for the takeover).

In the MECHA Constitution we find in the first paragraph their purpose, "To continue the struggle for self-determination of the

Chicano people for the purpose of liberating Aztlan." And in the Plan of Aztlan which MECHA is based upon, we find statements such as: "Aztlan belongs to those that plant the seeds,... not to the foreign European. We do not recognize capricious frontiers on the bronze continent. And "Brotherhood unites us...who struggles against the foreign "gabacho" who exploits our riches and destroys our culture."

This movement also known as "Aztlan" has been asked what is the closest ideology to theirs and they have said "Communism". Under "Economy" it further states: "Economic control of our lives and our communities can only come about by driving the exploiter out of our lives and our communities." And "Lands rightfully ours will be fought for and defended." And under "Self-Defense": "There will no longer be acts of juvenile delinquency, only revolutionary acts." (Think about what this means!).

Mexico has also sent millions of books for their illegal alien children in our schools in Spanish. The books teach the children the "Constitution" but not the American Constitution - the Mexican Constititution and also teaches the children that Mexico is taking back their land! There are MECHA Clubs now even in some elementary schools!

(It is also our opinion that many Chicano politicians in our system may be working for Mexican interests and not American interests; and others in high positions as well.) Calderon was correct when he said that "Where there is a Mexican (and was he including Mexican-Americans, also?), there is Mexico!"

Chapter 21

Just How Many Illegal Aliens Are in the United States?

The federal government continues to tell us that there are 12 million illegal aliens currently living in the United States. However, the actual number is undoubtedly five to six times higher.

The way the feds arrive at their numbers is as absurd as their assertion that we can maintain law and order without actually defending our borders.

In 1986, President Ronald Reagan granted amnesty to the nation's illegal alien population. At the time, we were told that population totaled between two to three million. However, amnesty was actually granted to five million who had crossed our borders illegally.

Washington arbitrarily estimates that every year since 1986, a half million illegal aliens take up residence in this country, either by over-staying their visa or by crossing into this country illegally. Additionally, they believe that the one million illegal aliens who did not qualify for the 1986 Amnesty (many were criminals), simply stayed anyway.

When you multiply a half million by 22 years, then add the additional million criminal aliens to the total, you have 12 million illegal aliens.

That is the figure which U.S. politicians pushing for amnesty constantly espouse. These same politicians have never taken the time to explain to us just how they came up with that figure.

However, the U.S. Border Patrol places a much higher estimate on the number of illegal aliens now in this country. For many years, the number of apprehensions at the border have averaged about one million. When you then use the very conservative estimate that at least three times that many got away, over 22 years, along with all of the people who never return home after their visa has expired, you get a much different number.

Using the Border Patrol's own data and considering the relative ease with which drug smugglers and illegal aliens make multiple crossings into this country, the more realistic number is much closer to 60-70 million.

This is why Obama wants to count illegal aliens in the 2010 Census. We will be told that granting citizenship to such a large group of people at once will be a tremendous boost to our tax base, and end our exploding budget deficits.

Of course, the vast majority of illegal aliens do not now, nor will they ever make enough money to even qualify for income taxes, they will simply join the 45 percent of Americans who currently pay nothing and our National Debt will continue to soar.

The real reason Obama wants to grant the mostly Hispanic population amnesty is to secure the votes that they would then have as American citizens. Obama believes that doing so would assure Democratic control of the White House and Congress for the next several generations.

With illegal aliens' (especially Mexican illegals') explosion in their population not only including those sneaking across our borders by the thousands daily, but also their explosion in birth numbers, those in charge of our government have not figured in Mexico's desire to dominate and rule for the "Reconquista" (the "Reconquest of lands owned by Mexico for only 24 years). Their "Spiritual Plan of Aztlan" (taught in our public schools) states under "Program": "Our struggle then must be for the control of our barrios,..., lands, our economy, our culture and political life." There appears to be no desire to assimilate and be part of our country – but instead to take over. And under this same "Plan" under the heading "Political Liberation" it states: "Where we are a majority, we will control." This is incompatible with our way of life of Americans living together, respecting each other and being American first – not one where one ethnic group dominates over all others!

Chapter 22

Solutions

Finally, we offer a few, painfully simple measures to stop the current invasion and expel those who have no respect for our borders, nor for our citizens from our ranks. Truthfully, if any combination or even one of the following actions were taken by our federal government, most illegal aliens in this country would leave, effectively deporting themselves.

1) Place the military on the border.

Rather than sending a few hundred National Guardsmen to the 2,000 mile-long border under orders to never stop anyone entering this country illegally, the way President George Bush did, if say 20,000 troops along with their tanks, helicopters, and U.S. Air Force over flights were utilized along the border (the same way we do for other countries), illegal entries would come to a screeching halt.

We could simply take the troops from Germany, where 30,000 U.S. troops are stationed or any number of other locations around the world and use our military to protect our border!

The Mexican border could and should be made a permanent duty station. This would allow the Border Patrol to full staff the official entry checkpoints which would greatly reduce the amount of drugs and criminals coming into this country.

2) Prison sentences for CEO's who hire illegal aliens.

Whether it is a landscaping company run-out of someone's den in Cicero, IL; a 30-unit independent hotel in Virginia Beach, VA; or a corporate giant such as Tyson Foods Inc., once caught with illegal aliens in their employ, the head of that company should spend the next ten years of their life in prison.

Additionally, a percentage of that company's profits commensurate to the percentage of their employees who are illegal aliens should be seized.

3) Cut off all federal funds to cities which continue or adopt 'sanctuary policies' for illegal aliens.

If a city such as Chicago, IL which has such a policy in place, refuses to cooperate with Immigration and Customs Enforcement by not allowing police officers to inquire into, nor report the immigration status of arrestees, shielding criminal aliens from notification and eventual deportation, their funds will be immediately suspended. No more federal money for roads, schools, no special grants, no construction projects funded with federal money...Nothing.

Only once all municipal agencies in that city are found to be in compliance, will federal funds be restored.

4) Require anyone registering a child in a public school to provide proof of U.S. citizenship.

Mexican nationals have been getting a free education for their children on the backs of American taxpayers for far too long. The practice has led to overcrowded classrooms, and 'English as a second language' courses in all of the border states.

The amount of money spent per child in public school annually varies from state to state, as well as district to district. However, it averages several thousands of dollars per child. Why should American taxpayers be subsidizing the families of illegal aliens?

If parents were required to provide proof of citizenship to register the child, many illegal aliens would simply leave the country. You take away the things that draw them here and most will deport themselves.

The state of California is now bankrupt largely due to years of allowing Mexicans to illegally move their families to the state. Overwhelmed with Spanish-only speaking children, they can no longer provide a decent education for American children.

5) Begin mass deportations.

Again, if you take away the goodies (jobs, free education, in-state college tuition, food stamps, Medicaid, etc.), most will return to

Mexico on their own. However, there will remain a number of Mexican nationals who will refuse to leave, a great many of them will be hardcore criminals (gangbangers, drug dealers, etc.). These human predators will only return home, if forcibly removed.

We have heard so many times that it is "impossible to deport 12 million people." First, the number of illegal aliens in this country is closer to 60 million, second, nothing is impossible.

As I said, most will leave after they are denied the services which they now steal with ease. The rest would be deported upon arrest for other crimes.

This is the same nation which defeated both Nazi Germany and Imperial Japan. This is the same nation which invented the airplane and the telephone. And, this is the same nation that can do anything which we choose to do.

We have the infrastructure, resources, and the right to deport as many illegal aliens from this nation as we want. The only thing we are lacking is a federal government with the courage to do it. We must change that and take back this great country.

If we do not, future generations of Americans will reside in a Third World nation, and it will be a mirror image of Mexico.

www.ingramcontent.com/pod-product-compliance
Lightning Source LLC
Chambersburg PA
CBHW021228280526
45784CB00005B/2014